I WAS A REFUGEE

SHUKRI ZAKI EL-DAJANI, member of an old Palestinian Arab family, is a refugee from his homeland as a result of the Arab-Jewish war that has been going on for the past 12 years. He eventually graduated from Victoria College, Alexandria, and also read economics at the American University in Cairo. Last year he came to Britain to study journalism on the staff of the Western Mail. He is 24 years old.

In the first of a short series of articles, he describes the terrifying events leading up to his family's flight from Jerusalem to Egypt.

By SHUKRI DAJANI

TODAY there are about 1,500,000 half-starved Christian and Moslem Arabs living in the battered tents of refugee camps scattered throughout the Middle East.

They are the victims of a war that broke out between the Arabs and the Jews in 1948 following the United Nations' decision to partition Palestine—a war that still goes on.

I was one of those who got away—and luckier than most.

At the time those who took refuge in the neighbouring Arab States considered themselves fortunate to be alive.

Yet they were soon to discover that their fate was one worse than death.

I am one of the people who

Members of the Arab League debate possible repercussions of the United Nations Assembly approval, in December 1947, of the partition of Palestine. The six Arab delegations walked out of the General Assembly in protest against the decision. They refused to recognise the vote and reserved freedom of action.

plosions and the chattering of machine guns.

Our schoolmaster ordered us to throw ourselves on the ground. We lay there in terror for many hours until we realised that there was no hope of a lull in the firing.

Then, sliding along on our stomachs, we were led by the teacher to the assembly hall. There we spent the whole night huddled on the floor and trembling with fear.

No family

All night long the teachers were comforting the younger children, exhorting us to find their parents. My classmates and I were wondering if we would have a home and parents to return to.

Next morning, under a shower of bullets, we were rushed into an armoured bus and at our own bomb-shattered

Machine guns—

16. The series of three feature articles entitled 'I was a Refugee' published by the *Western Mail* had considerable impact on its readers.

17. Guests of Irene the Dowager Countess of Plymouth at her mansion in St Fagans. Third from right is the author, followed by Elma Cole, Lady Rosula Windsor-Clive and the Dowager Countess Irene.

18. Receiving a post-graduate diploma at the Welsh College of Advanced Technology in Cardiff, South Wales in 1961.

PARLIAMENTARY PRESS GALLERY

ANNUAL DINNER

"GUESTS MAY AMUSE THEMSELVES BY
FILLING IN THE EMPTY BALLOONS BELOW"

THE LANCASTER ROOM,
SAVOY HOTEL,
LONDON

Friday, 24th April, 1959

AUTOGRAPHS

19. Autographs of Selwyn Lloyd, Hugh Gaitskell, Russian Ambassador J.A. Malik and other dignitaries attending the Parliamentary Press Gallery Dinner in London, 1959.

20. Foreign Minister Oscar Kambona visiting the construction site of the Mwananchi project while the author briefs the contractor.

21. The author briefing President Julius Nyerere on the Mwananchi project during his visit to the site. Editor James Markham is in the centre.

PRESS CARD

No.......... 149

................Shukri z el - Dajani..................

to whom this card is issued and whose photograph
appears thereon, is employed as a NEWS EDITOR

by THE NATIONALIST......................................

Valid until December 31, 1965

Passport No. ....(if any)

THIS CARD IS NOT TRANS-
FERABLE. IT IS AN IDEN-
TITY DOCUMENT AND
DOES NOT OF ITSELF CON-
VEY RIGHT OF ACCESS OR
SPECIFIED FACILITIES.

Signature of Holder :

....

Signed ....

Director of Information Services
Ministry of Information and Tourism.

22. The author's press card as News Editor with *The Nationalist* newspaper.

23. Members of the local and international press corps pictured with President Nyerere and Vice-President Rashidi Kawawa after the first parliamentary session following independence. The author is first from the right (kneeling) and Neil Conway is fifth from the right, same row. George Rockey is first from the left (standing).

All along, my contacts with James Fraser were maintained on a regular basis. I knew from David that he followed closely the progress I was making and would occasionally give directives regarding my programme. Though I used to go often to London to spend the weekend with my cousin Fayek, I never informed James, as I did not wish to infringe on his very busy work schedule nor to abuse his kindness.

It was always a great joy and pleasure to be with Fayek, staying at his flat in Hammersmith. Fayek and I were already close friends from the times we spent our summer holidays with our families in Heliopolis. We used to play squash together and were the table tennis champions of the Sporting Club for the men's doubles. Our characters blended well together. We shared the same values, likes and dislikes. On one of my visits to London, the Dowager Countess of Plymouth insisted I should contact her daughter, Lady Rosula, who lived and worked there. When I did so, Rosula invited me to dinner. I mentioned to her that I was staying with Fayek and she kindly extended the invitation to him as well, informing me that she would also invite her cousin, Lady Melissa. We spent a most enjoyable evening at her flat in Mayfair. She had prepared an exquisite three-course meal that we consumed with much appetite, considering that we had not eaten for the whole day. Our budgets were rather limited and free meals were always a heaven-sent occasion! So pleasant was the evening, we never realized it was past two in the morning when we departed. Though their ladyships offered to drive us to our residence, our egos made us decline the kind offer. Once on the street, Fayek and I discovered that the total sum of money we had between us was not sufficient for the cab fare. With no bus services at that hour, it meant having to walk all the way to Hammersmith. That was an evening to remember!

My relations with Fayek were maintained even at times when geographic distances separated us. He became a successful doctor but fell victim to cancer at a fairly young age. His passing away left a scar on my heart. I still often think of him and of the happy times we shared.

Events in London

Two events that occurred in connection with London need recounting. The first, humorous in nature, concerns Col. Slade Baker. He was on a visit to London and was kind enough to invite me to lunch at the prestigious Army & Navy Club. My travel arrangements and expenses were all taken care of thanks to James Fraser. I was extremely excited to meet Slade Baker who, after all, was my original mentor. I was curious to find out from him what feedback he had received regarding my training. Equally so, I looked forward to a real good meal that would compensate for my usual beans on toast or roast beef slices or at best a curry with rice. At the entrance of the Club, I had to give my name and was then escorted to the dining table, where I was very warmly welcomed by Slade Baker. He looked well and was in very good spirits. We had hardly exchanged a few words when the waiter came to take our order. Slade Baker told me that the Club's speciality was oysters and that I should try them. He then told the waiter to bring each of us a plate of six oysters. I had never eaten oysters before in my life and had never contemplated having to do so. Within minutes, we were served the 'giant' oysters. There I was, aping every movement of Slade Baker in the process of swallowing each oyster, while trying to suppress the agony from being reflected on my face. At one moment, I genuinely thought that I could not restrain myself from being sick. It was a painful and agonizing experience that I will never forget. He ordered a second plate of six oysters and was kind enough not to insist that I do likewise. I suffered from nausea for the whole day following that meal and have never again eaten oysters. That unintentional bad experience was compensated by the words of praise Slade Baker had for my work and equally so by the 'good impression I had given to all who came in contact with me.'

The second event was one that provided me with the rare opportunity of rubbing shoulders with the most high-ranking politicians as well as the leading newspapermen and journalists in Great Britain. James Fraser invited me to be his special guest at the Parliamentary Press Gallery Annual Dinner. I recall my trip to London to attend that event and how excited I was to participate in such a prestigious function. David Cole, who had never attended this function, briefed me on what to expect and provided me with information that James Fraser requested him to transmit to me, including that I would be seated at his table with political and press dignitaries and that we had to be attired in black tie. In this respect, I was assured that Mr Fraser's secretary would accompany me in the afternoon to rent the outfit which the office would pay for. I will forever be indebted to James Fraser for the care and attention he paid to ensuring that I felt at ease and comfortable in the alien environment for someone of my age and experience. He spared no effort in introducing me to many of the key figures and guests of honour including the Foreign Secretary at the time, Selwyn Lloyd, the leader of the opposition, Mr Gaitskell, and the renowned Russian Ambassador to the UK, HE Mr Malik. The highlight of the evening was when James introduced me to these dignitaries and, thanks to him, they autographed my invitation card. After dinner, James accompanied me in the same taxi to my hotel. He made a few remarks about how well I conducted myself through the dinner and how interested he was to follow my conversations and discussion with the other guests, who were all seasoned politicians and senior media officials.

Before arriving at my hotel, he told me that I would soon hear of major changes in the Kemsley Newspapers group, but that I should not worry, as it would not concern me. He underlined that this information was strictly confidential and that I shouldn't divulge it to anyone, including David.

Two weeks later, news broke out concerning the takeover of the Kemsley chain by the Canadian/British press tycoon by the name of Thomson. The group was renamed Thomson Newspapers. At the *Western Mail*, the Director-General Mr Kemsley was replaced by David Cole. In London, my mentor and friend James Fraser resigned. Little did I imagine that our dinner in London would be the last time for me to see this kind man, whose joy and pleasure was to provide young men and women the opportunity to develop and build their future.

As James said, with the exception of changing a few faces and switching some positions, work at the *Western Mail* continued. David was thrilled by his new job and immediately set out to introduce major changes and reforms, mainly in management and policies.

David remained a regular friend and my status as a friend of the family continued to consolidate. In fact, when I first arrived in Cardiff and established personal relations with David, we often had frank one-on-one discussions over a few drinks. It was on such occasions that he confided in me that his modest background was an obstacle for him to be integrated in the high society of the local community. His professional success certainly compensated partially for that uncomfortable reality which he never overcame. On my part, I told him that besides my ardent desire to become a successful journalist, I wanted to obtain a part-time job parallel to my training to enable me to relieve my father of the monthly financial allowance he was transferring to me each month. David agreed to such an arrangement, on the condition that it would not interfere with my training.

A couple of months after my arrival in the UK, I had met by chance Akram Saleh, a friend of my cousin Fayek, who worked with the BBC Arabic service in London. He told me that there was a very large number of Arab students in South Wales and he wanted to include in his weekly programme reports about them as well as interviews if possible. Arrangements were made for Akram Saleh to come to Cardiff, where I organized meetings with the representatives of the student bodies from the various Arab countries. Though I had no experience in broadcasting, thanks to the professionalism and encouragement of Akram, within no time at all, I was providing his weekly programme with contributions on a regular basis. Once my engagement with the BBC became official and some revenue was guaranteed, I sent a letter to my father thanking him for all the sacrifices he made and requested him to stop the monthly financial transfers to me. I well recall writing that letter and the joy and pride it gave to me. In fact, I told David about it and we celebrated the event by having dinner at his home with champagne, which his wife Elma served with generosity.

I expand my training

In spite of my extremely intense working programme with the newspaper and later with the BBC, I was determined to avail myself of the opportunity to advance my academic qualifications. I had discussed this matter with the Dowager Countess of Plymouth, who was very well connected with the hierarchy of the educational system. She was extremely supportive and within weeks she informed me that the Welsh College of Advanced Technology was giving a one-year course for a postgraduate diploma in teaching English as a Foreign Language. In principle, the participants had to be professional teachers and the course was limited to 15 students.

A mixture of good fortunes worked to my advantage. The Dowager Countess was very friendly with Dr Wynne, the professor in charge of the course, who was willing to accept me, provided that I would not take the place of a professional teacher. That year, there were only 14 applicants for the course, hence I was admitted. In retrospect, I believe the diploma I received for that course was my crowning achievement in the UK. It was an extremely difficult and demanding course where I found myself with professional teachers from 14 different countries from various parts of the world. Though I enjoyed good relations with the participants, I naturally felt different to their way of thinking and environment in general.

Attending the course until early afternoon, then rushing to the newspaper where I would finish work at midnight, was my daily routine for that year. In addition, I had to fit in time for my BBC recordings, which provided for my livelihood.

Many were the times that I almost conceded to the temptation of dropping the course. Thanks to the wisdom and support of the Dowager Countess, I was always dissuaded from taking such an action. On the day of my graduation, she came to embrace me after the ceremony and confided that she often had doubts whether I would persist with my studies. By the time I graduated, I was approaching the end of my training period. In fact, I had already acquired my status as a journalist. My feature articles were published under my own byline and I was also contributing editorials, whenever the subject matter related to developments in the Middle East.

An event that had a special impact on the readers of the newspaper was when I wrote a series of three feature articles titled 'I was a Refugee'. In fact, I recounted a combination of true stories, including my own, of the plight of the Palestinian people in the first person. The articles had a tremendous impact. Hundreds of letters were received each day by the paper from readers who expressed sympathy and support for the Palestinians. I was invited to address many societies and organizations, including the Rotary Club. I was also a guest at several secondary schools to talk about the subject.

David Cole was pleasantly surprised by the reaction of the readers and by the fact that circulation of the paper had increased due to the publication of the series. I was immersed by the consequential effect of the articles for almost one month and came to the conclusion that the Welsh people were passionate and sincere in their support of those subjected to injustice. In fact, throughout my stay in South Wales, I never felt lonely or a stranger. I found the Welsh warm, friendly and hospitable. They also loved their country and this was manifested in their strong sense of nationalism.

Learning from growing experience

I have to recount another significant event that occurred in my final days as a journalist with the *Western Mail*, which had a profound and lasting effect on me, both professionally and socially. At that time, the Middle East was undergoing major political changes. Regimes were crumbling down like paper towers. The wave of Arab nationalism was riding high with President Gamal Abdel Nasser of Egypt dominating the political arena and the whole region became almost subservient to his overwhelming power and charisma. At the time, I felt deep frustration over the impotence of the Arab regimes vis-à-vis the conflict with Israel. My anger was compounded by the inhospitable reception which the Palestinians received in the countries where they took refuge and by the almost hostile attitude they had faced wherever they went. All these elements subconsciously played a role in negatively affecting my objectivity in writing about the situation in the Arab world. As a consequence, I wrote an article about the struggle of power in the Middle East in which I predicted that King Hussein's monarchy would soon be toppled and that there would be a *coup d'état* in Syria and Iraq. Though my forecast for the latter two countries proved to be correct, that concerning Jordan was wrong from the essence. The lifelong lesson I learned from this experience was twofold. On the one hand, I realized the prime importance of conducting a thorough and in-depth study on the subject to be addressed and, equally important, always to apply strict self-critical objectivity in dealing with it. On the other hand, I realized the strength and power I possessed as a journalist and the effect and consequences my articles could have on the readers. A short time after the publication of the article, I received a phone call from the Jordanian Ambassador in London, the late Anastas Hananiya. He and my father were lawyers and friends in Palestine and his son David, who was at school with me in Jerusalem before the exodus, was studying medicine in England. The Ambassador expressed astonishment that I would write such an article. He advised me as 'a father' to desist from any such 'irresponsible' action in the future.

Several months later, his secretary phoned to tell me that King Hussein would be visiting London and that I was invited to attend a cocktail in his honour at the Embassy. I later learned that my article was brought to the attention of the King and that he wished to see me. Our encounter was unforgettable. At one moment, he appeared before me in the midst of the dense crowd. He called out my name in his husky voice while advancing towards me with a big smile and arms open to embrace me. He joked about my prediction that his days as monarch were numbered and asked me in detail about my future plan. His parting words were 'I know you did not mean anything bad and I look forward to seeing you in Jordan.' Following that encounter, I realized how fortunate I was to enjoy the friendship and trust of the King. Equally important, I discovered then the outstanding qualities of the King – wisdom, tolerance, kindness and humility. My respect for him grew tremendously over time.

East Africa beckons

Several months before my official training period was coming to an end, I sought the advice of David as to what to do in the future. He encouraged me to seek employment in the UK with one of the group's newspapers or to work for one of the Thomson Newspapers in East Africa. I told him my preference would be to work in the field to gain additional experience. He undertook to prospect the opportunities in this regard. It was on a week-end when I was invited to dinner at David's home that he broke the good news to me. To be exact, it was after dinner when we were having a glass of port in the sitting room that he called his wife Elma to announce that I had been offered a job with the *Daily Nation* newspaper in Dar es Salaam, Tanganyika.

The next day at the office, he informed me about the details of the offer. I was to report for duty within one month to the main office in Nairobi for a briefing of several weeks, after which I would proceed to my duty station in Dar es Salaam.

From that day, events moved rapidly. I wanted to spend at least two weeks with my father in Cairo en route to Nairobi. Days passed like hours. The process of making ready for departure was hectic and extremely emotional. One of the most difficult moments was bidding farewell to the Dowager Countess of Plymouth and Rowland. We had developed extremely close relations. I was considered as a fully fledged member of the family.

There were the Coles of course, and an endless chain of colleagues and friends to whom bidding farewell was sad and painful. Somehow, I had a feeling I would never see any of these people again in my life. My departure was by train to London, and I do not exaggerate when I say there were more than 100 people to bid me farewell at the station that was within walking distance from the office. The sight of all these friends on that platform as I was waving goodbye from the window of my compartment remains vivid in my memory to this day.

4

Heading to East Africa

The Land of 'Uhuru'

My overnight stop in London was a continuation of the emotional environment that was sparked by the memorable send-off I had had at Cardiff railway station. I was literally up all night with my cousin Fayek and the group of friends with whom we played poker during my weekend trips to London. In fact, now when I think of it, all of them were of Palestinian origin.

My flight to Cairo seemed endless. We had a stopover in Frankfurt and another in Athens. All I thought about was being reunited with my father, whom I missed terribly. I was also very much looking forward to seeing my sisters, my aunt and other members of the family. Although I corresponded regularly with my father, there were so many things I was anxious to know. I tried to imagine the scene of my arrival.

So many questions occupied my thoughts. Is my father still supporting the whole family, aunts, uncles, etc.? Are we being treated better by the host country and made to feel more at home? Will I be confronted by any surprises on the family front, illnesses or any other problems? Apart from these thoughts, my main concern was the little time I had to spend with my father before my departure for East Africa.

Reunion with the family

The sight of my father at the airport, with his charismatic smile and open arms, remains vivid in my memory. It was a loving and happy reunion that filled my heart with immense emotions. During the drive home, I bombarded my father with so many questions about himself and my sisters. He laughed, saying everyone and everything was fine and that I should only think of myself and my own situation. At the moment, I was so overwhelmed by our encounter that I did not realize the pertinence of his remark. In the evening, all the family met at our home. I was thrilled to see that everyone was in good health; yet, it was clear that the working and living conditions left much to be desired.

Once everyone had either left for their homes or gone to bed, my father proposed that the two of us have a chat on the balcony, if I was not too tired. It was a warm summer evening with an unusual breeze that made us both comfortable. We enjoyed the moment. Then, to my surprise and amazement, my father told me I should reconsider going to East Africa. He said it was far away and that he would prefer that I seek employment in the Middle East or even in England.

I was so stunned by his remarks that I did not react for some time. For several months, I had been so excited about the offer to work in East Africa and I thought my father would be both happy and proud of this achievement. All of a sudden, I felt totally void of any feelings. Admittedly, my sojourn in the United Kingdom was to construct a career and maximize on the benefits of that rare opportunity. However, the real driving force for all that I achieved was my desire to please my father. I was unable to understand whether my father's statement was due to his fear for my well-being or because he considered my job offer not suitable.

Sensing that I was perturbed, my father got up abruptly, telling me I should get some good sleep. He embraced me and said he was so happy to see me and extremely proud of me. Though I was totally exhausted, I tossed and turned in bed for some time, weighing up my father's comments. As I was falling asleep, the words that remained echoing in my ears were that my father was extremely proud of me.

Next morning my father and I went to the Heliopolis Sporting Club across the road from our flat. It was a monument from the colonial days. The director was a former British officer, who commanded the respect of all members through his style of management. We had an English break-fast on one of the terraces that overlooked the large swimming pool.

My father first teased me by recounting the time I was suspended from the club for misconduct for a few weeks during the summer holidays when I was schooling at Victoria College. Then, he said he owed me an explanation about his remarks regarding my going to East Africa. The reason was his anxiety for me being in a faraway continent that was alien to us. We had neither family nor friends in East Africa. Besides, he felt I had good job opportunities in the Middle East, so why opt for the unknown? Before I could react, however, my father told me he had spent a good part of the previous night thinking about his remarks and that he realized he had made a grave error. He said he admired and respected my courageous decision and that I had his full respect and blessing.

Departure for Nairobi

My departure for Nairobi a few days later was extremely moving and emotional. That was the moment when it dawned upon me that I was heading to distant and unknown territory, not knowing when I would see my father and family again. Though I was fairly young at that time, I ventured into uncharted territory without fear or concern about what awaited me. In retrospect, I often wonder whether my attitude was one of maximum self-confidence or a lack of maturity or perhaps a blend of both.

Arriving at Nairobi airport in July 1961 after a very long and bumpy journey, I became immediately aware that I was in a different world. An official from the *Daily Nation* newspaper was carrying a placard bearing my name that was totally misspelled. He was not particularly warm in his reception – clearly not enjoying the task he was given. During the drive from the airport to the city, I was the one who took the initiative in the conversation by asking more questions and seeking information, which he would normally provide to me as a total newcomer.

The car stopped abruptly in front of a building and I was told that we had reached my hotel. The driver remained seated while I got my luggage from the boot and entered the hotel, which was of a distinctly sub-average standard. The lobby was crowded by locals, who were consuming beer and other alcoholic beverages. Most of them were clearly tipsy, to say the least.

I was struggling to carry my king-size suitcase to the reception, when one of the ladies approached me, saying she was available and giving me her room number. Witnessing this, the receptionist told me that the woman was no good and that he could provide me with someone 'much better'!

It was late at night and I was totally exhausted, yearning to sleep. I was eventually given a key for a room on the third floor. The hotel had no elevator so I had to carry my luggage up the narrow stairs and through several corridors. The room was tiny and dirty with a strong stench of humidity. The bathroom facilities were non-existent: the shower did not work, the toilet was blocked and the washbasin provided only drips of water!

I was mystified – to say the very least – by the choice of hotel made for me by the newspaper. Then I recalled the remark made by the person who collected me from the airport; he expressed surprise that I was an Arab, since I was white-skinned and spoke English like the British ... I must have fallen asleep there and then for my only recollection was finding myself in bed next morning, fully dressed and quite oblivious of where I was. I realized I was late for my appointment with the editor so I changed my shirt, sprinkled a few drops of water on my face and rushed down to take a taxi.

My appearance was quite the opposite of what I had wished for and planned. The secretary of the editor was welcoming, though clearly surprised by my attire and not particularly clean state. I asked for the bathroom, where I enjoyed splashing water all over my face and my hair. When I returned, the secretary led me directly into the office of the editor, whom I will call 'GR'.

GR clearly wielded considerable authority with the management in London. He was a tall, well-built man oozing with authority and self-confidence. Contrary to my expectations, he never asked me about my trip or the local conditions I encountered. Instead, he wished to know why I chose to come to work in East Africa. Almost simultaneously, he asked if I was 100 per cent Arab. I guess the accumulation of my long trip coupled with the reception to date and living conditions I had encountered was a catalyst to my reacting rather angrily but with restraint to his questions and attitude.

I told him that I was 100 per cent Arab, that I received my education at the best educational institutions, that I was not used to living in slums or fifth-class hotels and that I chose to work in East Africa because I sought experience and wished to develop my career. I went on to tell him that only after my arrival had I discovered that my salary would not fully cover my bed and breakfast expenses at the awful hotel that they had booked me into and that, if my contractual conditions were not considerably improved, I would resign immediately and seek employment with another newspaper.

There was a deafening silence in the room for nearly a minute while the two of us gazed at each other. Instead of replying to me, he asked his secretary to call one of his assistants whom he requested to accompany me on a round of the premises and to introduce me to the staff. It was lunchtime when my tour was completed and two of the journalists I met asked me to join them for lunch at the New Stanley Hotel, which was within walking distance. Before leaving for lunch, however, I requested that the secretary of GR inform him that I wanted my case to be settled immediately and that I had no intention of spending another night at that infamous hotel.

The 90 minutes I spent at lunch with David Jones and Harry Ward provided me with a wealth of information. This assisted me considerably, not only in charting my direction with the newspaper but also in understanding the social fabric of the society I was to become part of. The two men had served in the British Army in East Africa until a few years ago when they terminated their tour of duty. Apparently, like quite a number of other ex-service men, they decided to remain in Kenya and worked primarily in the media, benefiting from their good knowledge of the country and the local language. David was a bachelor, while Harry was married to a Kenyan lady. They were extremely friendly and volunteered valuable information to me. GR was a racist. He had even tried to dissuade Harry from marrying his Kenyan girlfriend, warning him that such action would jeopardize his future. I was the talk of the newspaper. No one expected to see a white-skinned Arab, who was so British in his mannerisms and character. In East Africa, your skin dictated your categorization as European, Asian, Arab or African. I was a European because of my white skin and no one would contest that.

Both men were shocked that I was put up at the hotel where I spent my first night. In fact, David insisted I should move to his flat immediately. Walking back to the newspaper, I was oblivious to the conversation of

David and Harry. I was impressed with the information I had learned but was unable to comprehend many aspects of it. Surely David Cole and those of the *Western Mail* had conveyed to their counterparts in Nairobi my background and qualifications. I had so much trust in them that I had never even checked the salary I was offered, being certain it would be adequate and appropriate. Could it be that racism was so installed in East Africa that it overrode all other aspects? As soon as we entered the office premises, someone told me the secretary of GR was urgently looking for me. Before parting, David told me he would accompany me after work to collect my luggage and go to his apartment.

Things begin to look up

GR was standing behind his desk when I entered his office. He told me there had been a misunderstanding and that he had given instructions to rectify all matters. My salary was doubled, I received allowances like the European journalists and even my office space had been adapted to the new conditions. This meant I shared a room with a British journalist instead of being in the general newsrooms housing all the Asian and African staff.

To his great surprise, I posed no questions but thanked him for his decision. He seemed uncomfortable and uneasy as he went on to explain that my duty station would be Dar es Salaam in Tanganyika as originally planned. The only change was that I would remain in Nairobi for one month to take part in the coverage of the event on 14 August involving the release from prison of Jomo Kenyatta, the renowned Kenyan nationalist leader.

That evening I moved to David's flat. In fact, he had arranged for Harry, his wife and several other friends to come to dinner so I could already make local acquaintances. What a fine and welcome antidote to my initial reception in Nairobi!

During the coming week, intensive arrangements were being made to cover the story of Kenyatta. One of the team was designated to remain at the newspaper headquarters to gather and sub-edit the news that would be coming from the various journalists in the field. Despite my nightmarish experience upon arrival, I never dreamed that my debut in East Africa would entail covering an event as historic as that of the release of Jomo Kenyatta. In fact, I never imagined that political developments in East Africa would undergo such major and dramatic changes so as to mark the dawn of independence for Kenya, Tanganyika and Uganda from colonial rule.

The day of Kenyatta's release remains vivid in my memory. The attention of the whole world was focused on this event. Tens of thousands of Kenyans and citizens from other parts of East Africa flocked to the land of the Kikuyu to participate in this historic and very emotional event. For two days and nights, we worked tirelessly in shifts while sleeping and eating at the newspaper office.

When the event was over, a strange feeling immediately prevailed whereby Europeans spoke openly about the beginning of the end of their future in the country, while the Africans equally spoke about their imminent independence. GR voiced his fears that if the Kenyans ruled, the country would be in ruins economically and that Europeans would be persecuted. Though he was a very able journalist, I never understood how a reputable chain of newspapers such as the *Daily Nation* allowed someone like him to be at the head of what was a powerful segment of the national media. Prior to my departure to Dar es Salaam, I had a meeting with GR during which he clearly outlined what he expected from me, underlining that he would remain my direct boss. Clearly, he did not like me and I was warned by David not to succumb to GR's provocations, knowing that my fate was in his hands.

Arriving in Dar es Salaam

I was extremely excited about taking up my post in Tanganyika. I was one of some 20 passengers of the East African Airways Dakota plane from Nairobi to Dar es Salaam. I chose a window seat, trying to see as much of the scenery as possible. The person sitting next to me was the military attaché at the German Embassy in Dar es Salaam. He had been on home leave in Hamburg and seemed to be very happy to return to his duty station. He gave me an excellent briefing on what to expect and showed interest in maintaining contact with me. Our encounter, again, was an act of fate that had a positive impact on my career in due course.

The airport consisted of a short runway and a very small building comprising a few rooms that housed the passport and customs officers and the representative of the East African Airlines. Everyone was so friendly and informal that passengers had to seek the immigration officer to stamp their passports.

I was met by a short, smiling, bespectacled man attired in a short-sleeve white shirt, white shorts, white socks and black shoes. He introduced himself as Tony Dunn, the manager in charge of the operations of the *Daily Nation* in Tanganyika. He clearly knew all the officials at the airport, who rushed up to greet him. He had a friendly disposition from the outset, trying to assist me in carrying my luggage to his blue VW Beetle that was parked at the entrance of the building.

When I sat in the car, I felt relaxed and happy. What a pleasant contrast from my reception in Nairobi! I was enchanted by the friendly environment at the airport, sensing that I would have no problem in integrating with people whose nature seemed easy-going and hospitable. The drive to my hotel, named 'Etienne's', took nearly 20 minutes, giving Tony time to brief me on the country, the work, the weather, in fact, on almost everything.

Etienne's was a ten-bedroom, single-storey villa, which bore the name of its owner and manager. He was a Frenchman in his sixties who had come to Africa seeking his fortune. His wife had died at a fairly young age and he decided to remain where she was buried and abandoned the thought of returning to his native country. Speaking English with an extremely strong French accent, Etienne was a noted figure in the city, appreciated for his sense of humour and his willingness to offer help to anyone in need.

While the residents were almost all Europeans, the hotel was a very popular venue for all members of the society to meet at sunset for their drinks. Upon arrival, I was welcomed by Etienne himself, who gave me a hug and assured me that I was given the best room. Tony and I had a beer on the terrace with the compliments of Etienne. Tony told me we would have dinner together that night and then departed. I went to my room, unpacked and lay on the bed that was totally enveloped by mosquito netting.

My thoughts were about my father. I had written to him from Nairobi assuring him that all was well, never mentioning the reality of my experience upon arrival there. Now I had an urge to write to him about my first impression of Dar, its hospitable environment and, most important, that I felt safe and happy. I wasted no time in doing so and gave the letter to Etienne who promised to mail it immediately.

As promised, Tony arrived at exactly eight in the evening, still in the same attire. I, who had showered and wore normal trousers, a shirt and tie, felt overdressed. The first thing that he said to me was that I did not need a tie, adding that, next morning, he would take me shopping to acquire clothes that were the official 'uniform' for civil servants and people working in the private sector.

Our first stop was at the New Africa Hotel, located at the end of Independence Avenue. It had a touch of Spanish architecture, consisting of two storeys with wooden arches. On the ground floor, there was a huge terrace that overlooked the bay. As we walked in, Tony greeted most of those present, while an elderly man approached us with words of welcome and escorted us to a table with a view on the waterfront. Tony introduced me to the person as his newly arrived assistant. I was later told he was the proprietor, of Greek origin, who ran the hotel with his wife, son and daughter-in-law.

Even at that time, the weather was hot and humid and both of us were perspiring heavily. I then understood the practicality of the 'uniform', while observing that I was practically the only client whose outfit stood out like a sore thumb.

Tony recounted to me a bit of his own background. He too was an ex-British Army serviceman, who had spent many years of duty in East Africa. He liked the country and had no intention of returning to live in the UK. He described himself as a self-made journalist, whose professional success was mainly due to his love for the profession.

Apparently, he was fully briefed on my Nairobi experience, brushing the affair off as an act of ignorance and racism on the part of GR. I was quite taken aback by his remarks, wondering why he should volunteer information regarding his hostility towards GR to someone like me whom he had just met and who was an Arab. As the evening went by and we lost count of our sundowners, it became evident that Tony's relations with GR were strained, to say the least. Tony was senior correspondent for the *Daily Nation* in Dar. He was also the general manager of operations that included the publishing of a local daily newspaper in Swahili, a language he had mastered. A chain-smoker, like me at that time, he told me I could never have chosen a better period to be in Tanganyika for my career and experience as a journalist.

Witnessing the dawn of independence

I will never forget Tony's words: 'My dear friend, you and I are not only witnessing but are also an integral part of the dawn of the independence of East Africa.' Tanganyika was granted the status of responsible government in 1960, when Julius Nyerere became chief minister. My arrival coincided with the declaration of Tanganyika's independence in 1961, when Nyerere became the country's first prime minister. In 1962, the country became a republic with Nyerere as its first president.

That evening was so educational for me. I had the fortune of being briefed by a seasoned journalist and analyst on the political, social and economic situation in Tanganyika. It was the period when the Tanganyika African National Union (TANU), headed by Julius Nyerere, was declared the ruling party of the country, and would govern, following the declaration of independence that was due in less than a year. Tony explained to me how the inter-community fabric of the country had become much more friendly and tolerant. He foresaw an exodus of Europeans, who would not adapt to being ruled by an African government. At the same time, he anticipated a possible limited backlash against those who had been noted for their racism, whether Europeans, Asians or Arabs.

He was right on both counts. A fair number of expatriates left the country prior to and immediately after independence. The few months after independence also witnessed the deportation of a very limited number of persons, mainly Europeans. One case involved an elderly British retiree, who donned the flag of the newly independent Tanganyika on his dog! While he considered his act to be an expression of support and celebration, the authorities interpreted it as an insult to the state.

On my second day, I had an extensive schedule that included meeting all counterparts in the media, both in the government and private sectors. I was also taken to the headquarters of TANU where I met the secretary-general of the party, Oscar Kambona.

Our office premises consisted of a shabby, street-level area that housed the Swahili daily paper produced locally and a 20 square-metre space from which Tony and I operated. We shared one desk next to which was our vital source of operation, the fax machine. Within a week, I felt very much at home, on both a professional and personal level. My only problem was not having a driving licence. There was no public transport and though Tony assisted considerably, I often had to use taxis that were both scarce and very costly.

On my tenth day in Dar, I sat for my driving test, only to be told by the smiling British officer in charge that he was failing me for speeding in the city centre. Instead of waiting a month for the second test, however, he gave me an appointment within days, at which time I obtained my licence and liberty. I should add a note that I had never taken a driving lesson in my life! I learned through watching my friends drive.

Somehow, all doors were opened to me. The four communities – African, Arab, Asian and European – treated me with warmth and friendship. The charm of Dar es Salaam quickly grew on me. The city centre consisted of one road, Independence Avenue, with shops, hotels, coffee shops and bars on both sides. A few kilometres away was the main exclusive residential area, Oyster Bay, where all diplomats, senior officials and the bulk of the European community lived. Within this very limited perimeter, the inhabitants intermingled and interacted, greeting each other even when they had not been officially introduced.

The rhythm of life was endless activity, particularly for us working in the media. Political developments dictated alertness day and night. I developed good relations with three key figures in the circle of the media: George Rockey, who was Director of the Government Information Services and who later became press secretary to President Nyerere; John Hogan, Director of the United States Information Services; and Alan Gilmore, Director of the British Information Service. In time, the three became close friends, despite our age differential and their considerable advanced professional status. In fact, George became my mentor and assisted me considerably in charting my career at times of turmoil and need.

Settling in

My relations with Tony continued to grow stronger. He complimented me regularly on my good and hard work. In fact, he sent several reports to GR to this effect. We also had a good social relationship, which enabled us often to spend evenings and nights eating, drinking and sharing information and analyses about political developments.

One evening, Tony and I were having our sundowners at the New Africa Hotel when the owner inquired whether I was still looking for a flat to rent. Shortly after he left, Tony surprised me by asking if I would be interested in sharing his apartment in Oyster Bay that overlooked the ocean. I knew he was living with his girlfriend, a Hindu Indian woman called Rama, who was teaching at a public school. I had never met her but he often spoke about her.

Apparently, he met her in Mombasa and she decided to quit her family and join him, causing a major scandal for her family and community.

The next day, I was bidding farewell to my dear Etienne with hugs and assurances from my part that I would remain a regular customer at his restaurant and bar. In fact, his bar was a valuable venue where we met with leading members of TANU like Lucy Lamac and Bibi Titi. The former was an attractive young university graduate, who was a good and reliable source of information. The latter was a physically huge self-made hardline trade unionist, who wielded considerable power within the party. She had a magnificent sense of humour and could hold her drink better than most men.

Within three months, I was well established in Dar, both professionally and socially. I was made to feel much at home at Tony's lovely apartment, with its magnificent view on the bay. My love for the sea was crowned each night by the soothing sound of the waves breaking on the shore across the road. With no air conditioning, my windows were wide open while I lay in my bed, heavily fortified with mosquito netting. Though dressed in nothing but my underwear, I often had to take one or two showers during the night to counter the heavy perspiration caused by the intense humidity and heat.

Tony's girlfriend and I maintained a friendly and cordial relationship from the outset. She was an extremely discreet person whose presence I seldom felt. She did not accompany Tony to any of the official functions; hence, our encounters were quite rare.

Contrary to my experience in Nairobi, I encountered no professional or social barriers. In fact, as noted above, I had the fortune of being welcomed by all the communities and, most importantly, professionally, I was given the full privileges and credentials of a European.

One lived one's life to the extreme, both professionally and socially. Something was, almost always, going on from dusk to dawn. Reflecting back on my rhythm of life during that period, I find it hard to believe how I survived both physically and mentally. The hours one worked each day and night, the amount of alcohol one consumed, the meagre time one rested, would normally have rendered an elephant totally incapacitated. Fortunately, I was young, athletic and driven by a tremendous determination to succeed in my career. A parallel permanent driving force was my earnest desire to demonstrate to my father that I would not betray his confidence and trust in me.

The political arena in Dar was so complex and ever changing, being not only in a pre-independence period but also in a rapid process of preparing for self-rule. One was witnessing the metamorphosis of a nation and being part of the profound daily changes in people, structures and systems and, to an extent, even in mentalities.

To me, the process was exhilarating. I had established good relations with almost all the key members of TANU, including Nyerere or the 'Mwalimu' (teacher), as he was called, Rashidi Kawawa, who later became Vice-President, as well as many other prominent members of the European, Asian and Arab communities. Often I was intrigued by the fact that many of these people, particularly the Africans, who were so simple and modest in all aspects, would within months be the lords and masters of their country and hold its destiny in their hands.

I well recall the case of Mr Tomba, an anti-colonialist firebrand member of TANU, who was appointed Ambassador to the Royal Court of St James after independence. He was a man of extremely modest means, who must have found the abrupt change in status rather overwhelming. In this regard, I cannot but pay tribute to the Tanganyikans, who were exemplary in the manner they acted after assuming power. Their leadership demonstrated wisdom by calling for inter-community tolerance and unity. This was clearly manifested in the structure of the post-independence parliament.

Among the parliamentarians and cabinet ministers with whom I developed close relations were Amir Jamal, Nick Kassem (an Ismaili, who also represented the Aga Khan in Tanganyika) and Tulu Mueller, of German origin, whose parents came as missionaries and settled in the Arusha region.

To my surprise and amusement, I also came across two families of Palestinian origin. The Khourys were two middle-aged ladies noted for their social activities, particularly as regards the theatre and the arts. They had a brother who flew in and out of Dar on a regular basis and whose profession was a mystery never resolved. The other family, the Daniels, comprised two young men, who supported their retired parents. Destiny had it that I would meet up with the Daniels many years later in Beirut. Through their contacts with the church, they managed to obtain Lebanese nationality and set up residence in that country.

Each day, I realized the value and effectiveness of the training I had received at the *Western Mail* in Cardiff. My professional performance impressed Tony and key figures in the media, as well as the politicians and prominent personalities in Dar. Tony and I became noted for our scoops and for our ability to provide political analyses that had impact on the East African information scene. However, to everyone's surprise, and to that of Tony in particular, the unexpected occurred to put an abrupt end to our successful teamwork.

Transfer orders

Out of the blue, GR sent a telex to Tony, informing him that he had decided to transfer me to Kampala, where the *Daily Nation* had an office. Hard as he tried, Tony's interventions fell on deaf ears. It was at that time that he confessed to me that GR had told him from the outset that he planned to 'get rid of me' and that he would find a way to push me to resign. He intimated that GR was a known racist. I was dumbfounded by this revelation.

That night I lay in bed feeling dazed by the impact of the news. I felt so alone, so abandoned, despite Tony's support and understanding of the injustice being done to me. My financial resources were extremely meagre. I could not survive without a monthly salary. Resigning would play into the hands of GR – and that I would never do. I thought of my father, wondering what course of action he would advise. It was then that I overcame my doubt and loneliness; I was suddenly overwhelmed by a feeling of internal joy and strength. I decided to take the challenge: to go to Uganda, to take the new job and not to succumb to the schemes of GR.

An important element that I inadvertently omitted to mention earlier was that I had purchased an Alsatian dog that I named Kim. At that time, Kim was four months old and that was an added complication to my transfer. Tony was an animal lover, who welcomed Kim at his apartment and whenever my working hours prevented me from walking or feeding him, his girlfriend Rama undertook that task. The dilemma now was no longer my job but whether or not I should take Kim with me.

Early next morning, I phoned the hotel in Kampala and asked whether having a dog would be a problem. Much to my delight the answer was no, so I decided he would be my companion for the 1,700-mile journey from Dar to Kampala in my Mini Minor station wagon. Kim was surprisingly big in size, even for an Alsatian. Africans used to call him 'Simba', which meant lion, and feared him immensely. He was an affectionate and loving dog and I had much joy watching him as he developed into a formidable watchdog after training at the police kennels.

Tony, together with most of my friends, advised me against driving to Kampala. Besides the security risks, they pointed out that a considerable part of the road was not asphalted but consisted of narrow tracks. They were of the opinion that a Mini Minor was by no means the right vehicle for such a voyage and that my total lack of knowledge of car mechanics compounded matters. In an attempt to dissuade me, George Rockey made me meet a friend of his, Jimmy Feeny, who was a veteran of the East African annual car rally. Jimmy told me the idea was crazy and I would never make it.

Journey to Kampala

Reflecting on that journey to Kampala, I shudder even to this day when I think of the numerous dangers and risks I took. Somehow, in spite of all the warnings I was given, I was confident all would be well and had no fear of the unknown. It was a combination of ignorance, stubbornness and an urge for adventure that was my driving force. It was shortly before dawn that I set off on my 26-hour journey with Kim and a semi-automatic rifle that I had purchased specifically for the trip. My plan was to reach Nairobi early in the evening and then to proceed to Kampala at daybreak on the following morning.

The first leg of the trip to Arusha gave me a taste of what could and might happen. To achieve my timetable, I literally had to drive at maximum speed all the time, my foot pushing right down at full throttle. On numerous occasions,

I miraculously avoided collisions with other cars that were heading straight towards me as well as with individuals and animals, who suddenly appeared from the bush. A few kilometres before Arusha, I felt that something was wrong with the car. Upon verification by a mechanic at the only garage in town, I was told that the problem concerned the suspension that was on the verge of total collapse. There were no spare parts but the mechanic spent a good hour knocking things around, after which he assured me that the patch-up work he had done would enable the car to reach Nairobi but no further.

A major part of the route that I followed consisted of narrow tracks which were neither easy to follow nor to manoeuvre. I encountered more instances of people and wild animals springing out of the bush and often it was by the grace of God that we did not collide. I continued to drive at maximum speed, hoping that the car suspension would endure until Nairobi. It was just after sunset that I was back on the asphalted road and relieved to notice signs of some villages, though scarce and scattered. The most gratifying development, however, was that I was driving on 'normal' roads and, most important, there were signposts indicating directions – signs of civilization.

It was about ten at night when I checked into the New Stanley Hotel. The receptionist could not believe that I had driven all the way from Dar in one day in a Mini. He rewarded me with an upgraded room and 'exceptionally' agreed to allow Kim to share it with me. The first thing I did on the next morning was to phone my friends David and Harry from whom I had kept my transit visit as a surprise. They were extremely warm and welcoming. David volunteered to accompany me to the garage where I could have my car fixed. Harry kindly offered to have his wife take charge of Kim, allowing me to deal with my affairs in a speedier manner. The cost of repairing my car exceeded the sum of one month's salary. I had no option but to agree to what I considered an astronomical charge. The positive side was that the job would be completed within two days. Though I had no intention of passing by the office in Nairobi or of seeing GR, I found myself compelled to do so for financial reasons. I needed to take out a loan to cover the repair charges and for this I need the personal approval of GR.

It was after lunch when I went to see GR, who was surprised by my appearance. His lukewarm reception came as no surprise to me. I requested his approval for the loan, explaining the circumstances. While authorizing payment, he did not miss the opportunity to criticize my 'bad' judgement to go to Kampala by car. His only other remark was that I should report to duty in Kampala within two days at the most. David insisted I should leave the hotel and move to his place while Harry and his wife offered to host Kim during our sojourn, since they had a house with a garden.

At dawn of the third day, I set off for Kampala, feeling happy for the encounter with my two friends and more secure and confident that my Mini had been considerably overhauled. The road conditions for this sector of the journey were in any case much better. I made a few brief stops to allow Kim to run around and to have a break from driving.

At about nine in the evening, I arrived at the hotel in Kampala. I felt quite exhausted and, having checked in, I was pleasantly surprised to find myself in a huge colonial suite with a large balcony that overlooked the city. The next morning, I was collected from the hotel by the Director of the office in Kampala, a Mr Getty who told me that he knew my uncle in Beirut where he had worked for Reuters for several years. He briefed me on the activities of the office, emphasizing that it was a very small and limited operation. In fact, he expressed surprise that I was transferred to Kampala, as he had not requested additional staff.

It became rapidly clear to me that Mr Getty was going out of his way to assist me in settling down. On the professional side, he decided to give me part of his journalistic responsibilities and to concentrate more on the management aspects. In fact, we were the only two expatriates at the Kampala office. In view of the low volume of work, I was told to dedicate the first two weeks to finding lodgings, a task that proved more difficult than I had expected. There were very few small apartments in the security safe zones of the city and their rents were beyond my budget. Small houses, though costing less due to their location outside the city-centre perimeter, posed an increased security risk and many additional expenses.

Although I was quite happy working with Mr Getty and enjoyed a friendly work environment, I had an inner feeling that my stay in Kampala would not last for any length of time. After ten days, an Englishman who worked in the private sector contacted me to say that he had suddenly been recalled to return to the UK and that I could take his apartment, which was in an excellent location and was reasonably priced. His only condition was that I should finalize the contractual arrangements immediately to relieve him from his obligations in this regard. Getty thought it was a God-sent gift and urged me to take it without delay.

I spent a whole night agonizing, tossing and turning in bed, unable to comprehend my hesitation or in fact my reluctance to take up this golden offer. When I informed Getty in the morning that I had decided not to take the flat, he was evidently disappointed and quite bewildered. It was clear to me, to Getty and to all concerned that I could not get a better offer. Then why did I decline it? No one knew the answer, least of all me.

Recalled to Dar

It was exactly on the 14th day following my arrival in Uganda that I was awakened very early in the morning by a telephone call from Frene Ginwala, a noted South African journalist of Indian origin who was deported to Tanganyika allegedly for inciting activities against apartheid. Frene had become a symbol of South African nationalism. She enjoyed excellent relations with Julius Nyerere, Oscar Kambona and the TANU leadership, and was highly respected and admired for her syndicated articles that had a wide readership throughout Africa.

I had met Frene when I worked in Dar es Salaam and we had established a strong professional relationship. Before my sudden transfer to Kampala, we used to have regular long discussions at her apartment about the profound changes occurring in East Africa and how they would impact the entire region, including South Africa. I was always amazed by her political insight and vision and her unassuming character. Her life and soul were entirely dedicated to the cause of ending colonialism and, most of all, the apartheid regime in South Africa.

Frene's voice that morning was music to my ears, for she was a sincere friend. She had assisted me considerably in establishing key contacts and in providing me with valuable information and analyses when I first arrived in Dar es Salaam. She did not like or trust Tony Dunn, who had often told me she wielded formidable power in the political arena in Tanganyika.

She told me that she was shocked and very disappointed when she learned I had left for Uganda without informing her. For that, I was reprimanded for a few minutes, after which she told me she had my coordinates from George Rockey. In her typical style, she told me to pack up and return immediately to Dar. She said the government had decided to establish a publishing company to be named Mwananshi Publishing that would produce daily newspapers in English and Swahili. She had proposed my candidature to take charge of the operation and both Nyerere and Kambona had given their full approval. I was expected to be in Dar within a week at the latest. Frene never gave me a chance to react, ending her conversation by asking me to contact her once I arrived in Dar.

The whole conversation took no more than a few minutes. I was so perplexed that it took me some time to realize I was not dreaming or hallucinating. While I lay in bed, I thought of my father and of how I felt his blessing as a driving force and protection for me. Once again, my strong belief in fate was consolidated by this quite unimaginable turn of events.

My greatest pleasure and joy was to write my letter of resignation to GR. It was just a couple of lines, simply saying that I was resigning with immediate effect and thanking Tony Dunn and Mr Getty for their assistance. I handed the letter to Getty at around noon and informed him I would be heading to Dar the next morning. I did not mention anything about my future plans and he had the good discretion not to ask any questions. The next day, it was before dawn that Kim and I were in the Mini, heading back to the land of Kilimanjaro. Now I had my answer to the inexplicable inner feeling I had had that I would not last long in Uganda!

I was overwhelmed with joy at the thought of returning to Dar. It was as though I was returning to my home. What added to my happiness was the golden opportunity I had before me to develop my career and benefit from the rare possibility of living the events of the birth of a nation, while being in the inner circle of those who were the key players of the process. On the way, I found myself talking to Kim! All my anxiety about my Kampala posting, my professional frustration and my scepticism about all that was going on around me exploded in a tsunami of words that lasted for several miles. My verbal convulsion resulted in a strong feeling of mental and physical calmness and peace as though I had ejected an accumulation of venom from within my head and my soul.

I had decided not to contact anyone in Nairobi, not even my friends David and Harry, to avoid any embarrassment vis-à-vis GR. It was past one in the morning when I reached the New Stanley Hotel. My voyage had been quite uneventful. I was completely exhausted and needed to sleep before departing on the second leg of my journey to Dar.

I could not wait to arrive in Dar, to see George, John and other friends and of course Frene, who had become my saviour. I was equally interested to find out Tony's reaction to my new assignment. In effect, I realized that he and the *Daily Nation* would now need to go through me with regard to their relations with the top government officials and the local media.

I started my 15-hour trip from Nairobi to Dar at 4.30am. I was aware the 1,000 kilometres ahead of me would be much more arduous than the trip from Kampala to Nairobi, particularly due to the road conditions – in fact, due to the lack of real roads, as a major part of the voyage would be on 'marram' tracks.

It was a nightmare, driving for hundreds of kilometres where I also encountered rain that made conditions even more hazardous. Amazingly, however, it was neither the difficulties nor the dangers that left the utmost impact on my memory but a single event or happening that remains so vivid in my mind to this day. It was sunset when I was approaching the Arusha region and I made a stop to allow Kim to run around and to stretch my legs. Suddenly my view was directed, as though by magnetic force, towards Mount Kilimanjaro which majestically dominated the entire region. The phenomenal sight was that its snow-covered peak flowed with a magnificent red colour from the sun's rays.

I was so captivated and moved by this view that tears of joy came running down my cheeks. I recall thinking to myself, 'Here you are, a homeless ex-Palestinian refugee, all alone in the wilderness of Africa, in search of a future and security.' Kilimanjaro was according me a special welcome. To me, this was clearly a good omen; I was informed later by experts that what I witnessed was an extremely rare happening and that the locals consider it to be a sign of good fortune and a blessing. I proceeded with my trip, feeling happy and confident that what was awaiting me would compensate for the injustice done to me and the difficult times I had encountered.

A brighter future

The closer I came to Dar, the less I felt the fatigue and the more my spirits were elevated. As I drove up to Etienne's, I felt as though I had never left. My overwhelming joy washed away all memory of the Uganda episode.

As I entered the reception, Etienne appeared from nowhere and pounced on me joyfully – although as he gave me a hug, a puzzled look crossed his face.

Unaware of my several weeks of inferno, he expressed surprise and disappointment that I had not frequented his hotel of late. I was in no mood to enter into a discussion and responded by telling him I needed a place to sleep and that we would talk in the morning.

The next day, it was Etienne himself who gave me the honour of serving me breakfast in bed. It was nearly noon and he was clearly curious to know what was happening to me. Laughingly, he asked whether Tony and I had quarrelled and I had walked out of his flat. Clearly, he had not seen Tony during my absence and no one had mentioned to him that I had left for Uganda. I was feeling happy and naughty, so I let him suffer in his guessing. He loved gossip and always had a juicy story to tell. After pronouncing several scenarios, including the one that I had been involved in an affair with Tony's girlfriend Rama, he left the room saying he would find out sooner or later.

My first contact was with George. I felt I owed it to him to break the good news of my return and, more importantly, the reason. I had wondered in fact whether George might have known about my job offer, considering his relations with Nyerere and Kambona. The answer was no; the poor man almost had a heart attack when I appeared in his office! Hence, I decided not to talk about my job offer until my meeting with Frene Ginwala. He was very busy and we agreed to meet at his home for dinner. Frene looked regal in her colourful sari when she opened the door of her flat. She embraced me, saying it was good to have me back 'where you belong'. A phrase that still rings in my ears, for it was really the beginning of my professional maturity.

We sat on the large veranda of her fifth-floor flat, overlooking Independence Avenue. She did almost all the talking, giving me detailed information about the project, its inception and objectives. In a nutshell, the new African leadership wanted to establish English and Swahili daily newspapers to compete with the existing 'colonial' local newspapers: *The Standard,* the *Sunday News* and also the Kenya-based *Daily Nation.* This was to be achieved by setting up a publishing company that would produce the two newspapers as well as a wide range of publications in Swahili and English. I was to be in charge of the entire operation, which included building the premises, purchasing the equipment, appointing the staff and, in the process, setting up a school of journalism that would train young nationals in the various editorial and technical areas. The deadline for having the project fully operational was two years. During the preparatory period, I would have full authority and responsibility for all aspects. However, a member of TANU, Joeli Mgogo, would be responsible for all political decisions. Once the publishing company was operational, the editor-in-chief of the English paper *The Nationalist* would be James Markham, an ex-aide of the Ghanaian President Kwame Nkrumah, while Joeli would be editor of the Swahili daily *Uhuru*. I would assist James on the editorial side as well as my other responsibilities. Tulu Mueller, who was a member of parliament, with wide experience in printing, would be the technical director. He would advise on the equipment to be bought and the design of the building to accommodate it. In fact, I was made to understand that both East Germany and West Germany had offered to donate all the required equipment. Ironically, the only condition made by both governments was that they would not agree to have their machines in the same open premises and, more importantly, that their technicians should have no contact with each other. Tulu, who was of German origin, apparently advised that the Tanganyika government should opt for one of the two donations. Kambona thought otherwise. He decided to accept both donations, telling Frene that it was my job and responsibility to find a solution for the complex situation.

The two of us were so engrossed in our discussion and were oblivious of the darkness that fell around us. It was only when some visitors arrived that we became aware of the time. I rushed to the phone to call George, to excuse myself for being late. Before departing, I asked if I could mention my job offer to George; the answer was yes but with no details. Also that no one should know that Frene was in any way involved in the project. She informed me that a meeting would be soon arranged with Nyerere and Kambona at which my contractual conditions would also be discussed.

I drove like a bat coming out of hell to make up for my delay and found the Rockey clan waiting for me in front of their bungalow with open arms and the warmest of receptions. Miriam, a pretty lady from Seychelles, together with George and their two children Timothy and Kim, had become family to me. It was a happy moment and grand reunion for us all.

Again, things seemed to fall in place as though I had never been away. We sat at the bar to have our customary drinks while Miriam slipped away to the kitchen to finalize the dinner. They all asked about Kim, the dog – we always had to say that to differentiate from Kim, the daughter! I assured them that he was being well taken care of at Etienne's. My statement brought anger from adults and children alike; they insisted I should be their house guest and that Kim the dog would be much more at home in their garden and with them rather than at Etienne's. Dinner was served soon during which we spoke of everything but work. Within minutes of finishing dinner, Miriam and the children disappeared leaving me and George with our glasses of cognac. 'OK my boy, let's have the whole story. I am all ears,' were the resounding words of George.

I spoke very briefly about my Uganda experience. I did not wish to open old wounds nor did I think that it would serve any purpose. Knowing George, his main interest was to know what had brought me back. I very much realized that I had to be careful about how I presented the situation regarding my job offer, knowing how sensitive he was, particularly with regard to his profession and his relations with Nyerere. I recounted to him all that Frene had told me, but omitted all mention of Nyerere and emphasized the fact that nothing would be final until the approval of Nyerere was obtained. I concluded by telling him that Frene was playing the role of go-between at the request of Kambona.

It took George some time to react. As I expected, the expression on his face was one of satisfaction but with a degree of puzzlement. He said he was very happy for me to be chosen for such a key post at that juncture of the history of Tanganyika and was confident that I would do a good job. He expressed surprise that he had heard nothing about the project and intimated a degree of anxiety that Kambona may be acting singularly without consulting the 'Mwalimu' (Nyerere). We had more glasses of cognac than I can remember. I eventually convinced him to call it a night, but only with the firm promise that I would move to his bungalow with my Kim until such time as I would find a residence. George was an honest, trustworthy and sincere man whose friendship I treasured. While he bid me farewell with his customary embrace, I had a feeling of deep anguish for my inability to recount all that Frene had said. My only consolation was that I had saved him the agony of discovering that Nyerere had purposefully or by sheer negligence omitted to mention the project to him.

The next morning, when I informed Etienne about my departure, the poor man was dumbfounded. On arrival, I had mentioned to him that I would need a room for a minimum of one month. His parting words were that he would not have a room for me, if I came knocking on his door within days. He was pulling my leg. As he waved me goodbye, he cried out 'au revoir' several times.

By noon, I was well installed at the Rockeys together with Kim the dog who was rejoicing hysterically in his new home, running all around the large garden. I spent my afternoon at the bungalow alone. I needed some time by myself to analyse the developments and my situation in an in-depth manner. Everything was moving so quickly, giving me little or no chance to evaluate the multiple events. In the coming few days, I would need to make decisions and commitments that would have far-reaching effects on my future.

I recall sitting down to write a letter to my father. I was impatient to inform him about my recent job offer and, though I had not finalized signing the contract, I needed to explain to him my feelings and share with him my joy and my anxieties. I thought of what lay ahead for me. The vast responsibilities, the intricacies and complications of the job and, most importantly, my relations with members of the media, both the locals and expatriates.

When Miriam and the children returned late that afternoon, I had already planned for my expected meeting with Kambona and Nyerere. On the professional side, I had a fairly long list of conditions, most important of which was assurance that I would have full authority of action and that I would have easy access to Kambona, who was my counterpart for the project at the government level. With regard to my contractual conditions, experience had taught me the need to have an inclusive agreement that would cover all aspects of my requirements and that my remuneration should be commensurate with the level of the post and its responsibilities. I was thirsty for work and had confidence that I would succeed but I needed peace of mind and financial security as a foundation to achieve this end.

I had to telephone Frene to inform her that I had moved to the Rockeys. She alerted me that the meeting with the TANU officials was imminent. I should mention that at that time, Nyerere was already Prime Minister and Kambona was Minister of Foreign Affairs. Ironically, during this transition period, it was their party status that wielded and exerted power. Perhaps it was the presence of the British Governor-General and the lack of full independence that created this unusual situation.

We were in the midst of our dinner when the phone rang. George informed me it was Frene on the line. She was telegraphic in her remarks; I should be at her place within half an hour for the expected meeting. The short notice took me by surprise, but within minutes, I was driving along the coastal road towards town. Frene was waiting at the entrance of her building and hurriedly got into the car. She guided me to a villa that I later knew to be Kambona's home.

Kambona opened the front door himself and was extremely warm with his words of welcome. He wasted no time in discussing the purpose of my visit. In fact, he said the 'Mwalimu' would arrive any minute and he wished to ensure that we were in agreement on all matters prior to his joining us. I responded by telling him I had prepared two papers containing my contractual and operational conditions, both of which I submitted to him. Without taking a glance at them, he said he agreed to whatever conditions I might have. He underlined the importance of the project and its success for the country. At this point, he received a signal that Nyerere was about to arrive and hurriedly went to receive him.

Nyerere embraced me upon entering. He briefly told me about the need to have the project completed soonest and assured me that everything necessary would be made to facilitate my task. I mentioned to him the urgency of adequate accommodation and he instructed Kambona to attend to that immediately. He confirmed to me that Kambona would be ready to provide me with whatever I wanted.

Nyerere was a statesman, comparable in many ways to Nelson Mandela, whom he supported and exerted every effort for his release from prison. He was a soft-spoken man for whom I had a great deal of respect and admiration. Little did I imagine at the time the profound effect Julius Nyerere would have on my human and political moulding that took shape in future years.

It was clear his meeting with me that evening was a formality and a gesture to demonstrate the importance of the task I was to undertake. Our encounter lasted around 15 minutes, after which Frene and I left with the agreement that a meeting would be held with Kambona on the next day to finalize my contract and begin action on the project.

Supporting nationhood

That encounter, in fact, marked the beginning of a major change in my life, professionally and personally. From that moment in time, I became a recognized player in the development of the national media and a confidant of the political leaders, who gave me a free hand in dealing with matters that often went beyond my terms of reference and even my area of specialization. It should be recalled that Dar had become the hub of African nationhood at that juncture. The leaders of liberation movements such as Hastings Banda of Malawi, Kenneth Kaunda of Zambia, Joshua Nkomo of Zimbabwe, Eduardo Mondlane of Mozambique, to mention but a few, all worked out of Dar to promote their claims for independence and were given the full liberty of movement and speech to do so. I had the opportunity to interact with these leaders in close and private sessions, and therefore to witness at first hand the beginning of the end of British colonialism in Africa.

As already mentioned, Frene was a refugee from South Africa. She had to flee to Dar in the latter part of 1960 together with the Deputy President of the African National Congress Party Oliver Tambo and Dr Yusuf Dadoo. Here, they had established an office for the ANC. She had played a tremendous role in establishing underground escape routes for ANC leaders and cadres following the Sharpeville massacre. During the entire period of her exile, she traversed the world preaching against the horrors of apartheid and for the fight against it.

Frene, who was born in 1932, was a South African from the Parsi-Indian community. She had a doctorate in Philosophy from Oxford University and was a barrister at law, a historian and political scientist. Her dedication to the cause of African nationalism earned the respect and admiration of the entire leadership in the African continent. She returned to South Africa in 1991 and served as Speaker of the National Assembly during the period 1994 to 2004. I believe the exceptionally strong relationship I had with her stemmed from the base of being refugees who had to flee from our countries. We had so much in common with regard to our suffering and status of deprivation as well as our goals and aspirations.

Within a week of meeting Nyerere, I was allocated a magnificent two-bedroom bungalow that was located next to the Rockeys. Coincidence had it that my move to the new residence would entail settling some

75 metres from where I was already staying! I was provided with a cook, a houseboy and a gardener, who were loyal and efficient. Security was an issue, but I never had any problems thanks to Kim and my dedicated staff.

During the first few weeks, I worked relentlessly to formulate a comprehensive plan of action for the project. The TANU member responsible for political matters, Joeli Mgogo, was a nice person who was educated in East Germany and headed the national broadcasting services. He made it clear from the outset that he would be there when required but did not wish to be involved in daily affairs.

Tulu Mueller was my right-hand man. The two of us had worked with the architects to choose the premises and design the buildings. We then embarked on negotiations with the West and East German governments to obtain the printing presses. The military attaché at the West German embassy whom I had met on my first flight from Nairobi to Dar played an important role in facilitating our task with the officials in Berlin.

Concurrently, I was working on finding premises that we could use as a school for training journalists. Ironically, the most suitable place was literally next to the office of the *Daily Nation*. Clearly, destiny had it that I should be Tony's neighbour and competitor. When my assignment became public knowledge, all the foreign journalists and media officials flocked to congratulate me. Tony was among the first to visit me. He appeared to be genuinely happy for me and we continued to maintain friendly relations throughout my stay in Tanganyika.

I should mention that four months after my assuming the new post, Tony contacted me to say GR was in Dar and wished to see me. Our encounter was brief. He asked me to arrange a meeting with Nyerere or Kambona for him. I told him that he should contact George Rockey for that, as he was the official government press officer. He said he wished to see me alone for lunch or dinner to 'explain matters'. My response was curt but with a smile, saying there was nothing to explain. That was the last time I saw GR, though he never ceased to try to contact me either directly or through Tony.

Within two months, Tulu and I visited East and West Germany and concluded deals for the provision of two complete sets of printing presses. The arrangement was that they would be housed in the same premises but separated by a concrete wall. Within three months of the launching of our operations, a ten-metre opening was made in the wall and the East and West German technicians were mingling and having their sundowners together! It took a lot longer for the bigger wall in Berlin to come down … Joeli could not believe his eyes when he saw this happening. He always boasted that this was one of the historic achievements of Mwananshi Publishing Company.

The interest of Nyerere and Kambona in the project never ceased. In fact, both made regular visits to the site during the construction period. I recruited Neil Conway, an Irish journalist, as sub-editor. Along with me, he undertook the training of some 20 nationals that formed the team of reporters for the English daily, *The Nationalist*. Several months before the opening, James Markham arrived. He was a stocky, spectacled man in his fifties, a good writer and a seasoned politician, who hit it off very well with Joeli, as they both enjoyed a good drink at any time. James's wife, Joyce, was employed by Kambona as his personal secretary. The couple clearly enjoyed the confidence of the key politicians and I found working with them pleasant and effective.

In the meantime, Nyerere became President of the newly independent republic of Tanganyika and he appointed George as his Press Secretary. The Vice-President was Rashidi Kawawa. It is interesting to note the fact that Nyerere had officially proposed postponing the independence of Tanganyika until Kenya and Uganda gained their independence in order to maintain the structure of the Common Services that existed between the three East African countries. His condition was that the British government would set a short deadline for the independence of the two other colonies. This did not happen.

Months passed as if they were hours. I was so engrossed in my work that I had little time for my personal affairs. I maintained regular contact with George, who was always extremely supportive and encouraging. The two of us met regularly with John and Alan who never stopped trying to extract information out of us for their respective governments. Frene was far less involved in the project than I expected. We used to meet almost every week. I used to brief her on developments but our discussions focused more on the political scene and its fast-changing facets. Frene's syndicated articles were gaining wide readership throughout Africa and she had become a leading columnist in the magazine *Jeune Afrique*.

Notable encounters and events

My deadline of 24 months to have the project operational was maintained. In fact, the official launching of the company took place after 23 months. It was a national occasion for celebration. The President, the Vice-President as well as members of the cabinet, parliamentarians and TANU officials attended the opening ceremony. Nyerere made a speech in which he said that the English and Swahili daily newspapers published by Mwananchi would be the beacon to disseminate the legitimate opinion of the independent state of Tanganyika and its people.

I was overwhelmed by the number of people, including Nyerere, who paid tribute to me. I wished my father had been with me to share these moments of achievement and joy. Not quite 28 years of age, I had become part of the socio-political fabric of the country. I had earned the respect and trust of the leadership both at the political and community levels. I became identified as a friend of the nation, so much so that I felt totally at home just as I did in Palestine before the diaspora. In fact, the years I spent in Tanganyika were a blend of some of the happiest times of my life and an extraordinary opportunity to develop my career and my political vision.

It is painful for me not to recount all that I encountered during my years in Tanganyika. However, I will focus on the key events and incidents that had a major impact on me and which remain extremely vivid in my mind.

Collaborating with the Mwalimu

The first of these was my first encounter with Nyerere at the State House after he assumed the presidency. The meeting was arranged by George, who had become my mentor. I was warmly greeted with words of praise for what I had achieved for the country's 'free' media. It was at that moment of pomp and protocol that the reality of the change in the status of Nyerere became evident. Ironically, the man himself had not changed in any way. In fact, his attire was unchanged: a colourful shirt hanging over dark grey trousers and the traditional sandals. Nyerere indicated that he would occasionally 'use my political acumen' to publish editorials in *The Nationalist*. That arrangement was a state secret known only to the three of us attending that meeting.

In the course of my work, I was called to the State House several times to meet with Nyerere who, together with George, would brief me on the political direction they wished our editorial to follow the next day. This occurred at times when major political issues would arise. Nyerere wanted to convey a clear message without signs of his involvement. In fact, the idea was to keep foreign governments as well as local politicians wondering who was dictating the policies. Whenever this happened James, Joeli and Kambona would be told that the editorial was passed to me by George.

This situation worked as Nyerere wanted. Rumours circulated that Kambona was imposing his policies in complicity with James. Others thought it was Joeli with his East German sentiments that prevailed, or that it was George who was the author using his influence on Nyerere. Nobody guessed the reality that Nyerere was the source and that I was the executor, not even John and Alan, who were among the most seasoned diplomats and whom George and I met with regularly.

Revolution in Zanzibar

On 10 December 1963, Prince Philip (in the name of Queen Elizabeth) transferred power and authority of Zanzibar into the hands of the young Sultan Sayyid Jamshid bin Abdullah Al Said. The little island had witnessed decades of tension between the African population and Zanzibaris of Arab origin. This was manifested by the very divergent policies of the two ruling political parties, the Afro-Shirazi Party led by Abeid Karume and the Zanzibar Nationalist Party headed by Muhammad Shamte Hamadi, who was the Prime Minister.

Almost one month to the day following the transfer of power, a 25-year-old semi-illiterate bricklayer and painter by the name of John Okello, aided by former police officers and friends, staged a *coup d'état* that ousted the Sultan from power. The event that took place on 12 January 1964 stunned neighbouring Tanganyika, Africa and the entire world. The Sultan and his family, as well as the Prime Minister and members of the cabinet, fled by sea to Dar es Salaam, as a first leg of their journey to the United Kingdom where they sought political asylum. In the aftermath of the coup, thousands of Zanzibaris of Arab origin were massacred, while the world looked on with impotence and lack of action. The Arab League's action was limited to a statement of condemnation. Tanganyika, which traditionally had close contacts with the Afro-Shirazi Party and Karume, lost no time in establishing contact with Okello, who had bestowed upon himself the rank of Field Marshal. He also gave the rank of General to several of the friends who aided him.

At this juncture, I need to recount an incredible personal experience I encountered in relation to that event. When news broke out that a coup had occurred in Zanzibar, my first instinct as a journalist was to immediately go there to cover the event. Strangely enough, it was Neil Conway, who worked also as freelance journalist for the Associated Press, who was the first to be alerted by his agency. We agreed to charter a Cessna aircraft to take us to the island. Within an hour, we were ready to take off for Zanzibar, piloted by Tim, the Irishman, who owned the charter company 'Timair'.

It was a clear day with a magnificent blue sky and a sea below that resembled a lake in its stillness. We were flying at a fairly low altitude, watching some dhows sailing towards Dar. It was only then that Neil told Tim about our mission and about the unknown reception that awaited us. The conversation that ensued between the two Irishmen during the first ten minutes of the flight centred on the risk factor of damaging the aircraft. Tim indicated several times that he should have charged us double the amount. Zanzibar was soon in sight and Tim was busy trying to establish contact with the tower for permission to land. As our altitude was decreasing and we were getting closer to the island, Tim was getting very irritable and nervous, saying he would turn back if he had no response from the tower within a few minutes. Neil and I were urging him to continue his descent. We told him the situation was chaotic and there was probably no one at the tower to answer. Tim finally agreed that he would fly over the runaway at a fairly low altitude so we could physically see what was going on, while he continued trying to establish radio contact.

While approaching the runway, we could see a lot of movement at the airport; there were men running around all parts of the very small airport and vehicles were moving in all direction at high speed. Suddenly hell broke out. Machine-gun fire was targeting us from all directions. To this day, I can never forget the reaction of Tim, who pulled the small plane up sharply to an almost vertical position to gain altitude, while exploding in a stream of insults directed at Neil and myself. And he never ceased calling us all sorts of names throughout the 20-minute return journey!

Before landing back in Dar, he told us that the fuselage had been damaged and we would be lucky to land safely. Both of us thought he was deliberately trying to dramatize the situation. In fact, eight high-calibre bullets had pierced various parts of the aircraft, as we noted upon landing. We could hardly believe what we saw and embraced each other in a mixture of relief and exhilaration. We spent a good half hour at the hangar sharing a bottle of whisky, which Tim supplied, and counting our blessings for the miraculous escape we had from what could have been a fatal incident.

Again destiny and fate had it that I should not only survive this event but, more importantly, that we did not land in Zanzibar. Little did I know at the time that the *coup d'état* was meant to eradicate the Arab community. Had we landed, my fate would doubtless have been like that of the thousands of Arabs, who were hacked to death by 'pangas'.

The leadership in Tanganyika was in a state of emergency. There was major concern that the trouble on the neighbouring island would soon spill over to the mainland. Early that evening, I was informed that Kambona wanted to see me at his office. I had never seen him so sombre. He questioned me in detail about my Zanzibar adventure. He had a couple of men who literally interrogated me about all I had seen on the island. They wanted to know the approximate number of people at the airport, the number of vehicles and even their shape and size. Clearly, they were from the intelligence unit.

I was extremely astonished when Kambona spoke about his intended visit to Zanzibar the next day. Almost immediately after that revelation, he thanked me and while leaving, I was told by one of the two persons not to mention what I heard to anyone. Later, it became known that he was chosen by Nyerere to go to the island in order to make sure matters would not get totally out of control. The plan was that Kambona would try to convince the coup leaders to accept troops from Tanganyika to help them stabilize the situation. The other aspect was to ensure the security of Karume, whom the leadership in Dar wished to install in the number-one position in due course.

Kambona's mission was successful beyond expectations. Not only did he get approval for Tanganyika troops to be immediately deployed on the island and have Karume acknowledged as the civilian leader but he miraculously managed to fly back to Dar accompanied by John Okello. In the weeks that followed, I was told by Kambona himself that the most crucial part of his mission was to get Okello off the island. Kambona asserted that the self-appointed field marshal would never be allowed back and that Karume would eventually be declared head of state.

That is exactly what happened. Late in January 1964, Abeid Karume was declared President of Zanzibar. Developments occurred more rapidly than expected. On 25 April in the same year, we witnessed the birth of 'Tanzania', uniting the island and the mainland into one state with Nyerere as President and Karume as Vice-President.

A historic incident which I experienced was meeting John Okello by chance at the office of Kambona. It was a few weeks following his arrival in Dar. He was in the waiting room, sweating heavily and extremely agitated. Kambona's secretary, Joyce, welcomed me and ushered me in immediately. Okello rushed to her saying that he was there before me and should not be made to wait. I was astonished by her attitude when she ordered him to sit down and to keep quiet, a command to which he immediately acquiesced.

I was dumbfounded by what had happened and I took the liberty to ask Kambona what was going on. He told me, confidentially, that Okello was being sent the next day to Uganda, his country of origin. Smiling in his usual manner, Kambona asked whether I would have ever imagined someone like him could execute a successful *coup d'état*. When I came out of Kambona's office, I sat in the waiting-room for nearly 15 minutes watching and observing this sturdy young man who made history by reshaping a country. The question I asked myself then and I continue to ask now is whether this helpless, lost person could ever have been the mastermind and leader of the coup.

The army mutiny

The first six months of 1964 not only witnessed the coup in Zanzibar and the birth of the state of Tanzania but another event that could have had dramatic consequences for the whole of East Africa. That event was the mutiny of the army.

In January 1964, following the unrest in Zanzibar, there was a mutiny in the Tanganyika Rifles, the sole regiment in the Tanganyika army. Nyerere, who went into hiding with Kawawa, appealed to the United Kingdom to intervene. The aircraft carrier HMS *Centaur* was despatched from Aden to stand off the shore of Dar. Royal Marine commandos were landed by helicopter at the capital on 25 January, assaulting and quickly capturing the barracks. Many of the mutineers surrendered after a guardroom was destroyed by an anti-missile tank. The mutiny that had spread to Tabora and other parts of the country was brought under control in five days. In the meantime, the mutiny had spilled over to Kenya and Uganda but swift action by both countries ended the unrest within days, following intervention also by British troops.

In April 1964, 19 African soldiers of the Tanganyika army went on trial before a special military court. I attended all the sessions. They were unanimous in their testimonies. Their intention was not to topple the government or hurt anyone. Their action was merely to express their deep grievances about the protracted process of Africanization of the army. Two years had elapsed since Uhuru (independence) and there were still almost 50 British officers and NCOs in the army that remained under British command. They also complained that their salaries were too low and that their repeated request for an increase was disregarded. Listening to their testimonies day after day and observing their attitudes, reactions and responses, I had the impression that these young able-bodied soldiers were not aware of the seriousness of their act nor of its far-reaching consequences.

Several months later, at a private evening with Kambona, the subject of the mutiny came up. He confirmed to me that he had in fact gone to the barracks and met with the 'coup leaders' to negotiate a settlement. According to his account, two of the soldiers dominated the rest whom he described as fairly passive and agreeable. The two militants were not willing to make any concessions nor compromises and he considered himself lucky to have been allowed to leave. Kambona did not mention to me the demands of the two mutiny leaders. His version was that his advice to Nyerere after that meeting was to request foreign intervention. I well recall that when Nyerere came out of his hideout, he publicly thanked Kambona, whom he called 'my colleague', for defusing a potentially dangerous situation.

Tragic accident

It is traumatizing for any person to experience a mutiny at first hand. To me, that event was one of the most haunting and difficult to endure to this day. I was at the newspaper office, which was located a few kilometres out of the city centre, in the direction of the airport. James received a telephone call from Joeli telling him that everyone should immediately go home as there were serious problems in Dar and that gunfire could be heard throughout the city. Panic struck and all the staff were scurrying to leave the building.

It was before midday, none of the German technicians had arrived and Neil Conway was on sick leave. I got to the phone to contact George whom I thought was the best-placed person to provide concrete information on the situation. His line was dead. I persisted for a while, as temporary rupture in the communications systems was not an uncommon occurrence. After about 15 minutes, I abandoned my attempts. I was suddenly struck by the stillness and complete silence all around me.

The immense building that housed nearly 150 people was literally void of any sign of human life. I looked out onto the car park and saw my small white Simca car conspicuously solitary in the large area in front of the establishment. As I hurried to leave, I was surveying whether anyone was still there. It was a ghost building, as though never inhabited. It was hard to believe or imagine that all the employees, men and women, had evacuated within such a short space of time and that I had been oblivious to that massive exodus while on the phone.

I headed towards town, which I had to traverse to reach my home. I observed large numbers of men and women on both sides of the road, running away from the city. My car was the only one on the road and, having covered less than a mile, I could hear the sound of gunfire in the distance. I had no option but to continue if I were to find a safe haven. I well recall the scene, which remains so vivid in my mind; the crowds getting more dense and panicky as I progressed on my way toward the little bridge which I had to cross. I had to reduce my speed considerably to pass over the bridge, which could only accommodate one car at a time and had extremely narrow pavements for pedestrians on both sides. By the time I was at the beginning of the bridge, the crowd of fleeing people was so dense that I had to almost stop. I was among a sea of African men and women scuffling to cross in the other direction, involuntarily banging into all sides of my car. So dense was the crowd that I could not see the road in front of me.

As though from nowhere, a man bounced onto the bonnet of the car and came hurtling towards the windscreen. I recall crossing my arms to protect my face from the human projectile. There was an astounding explosion. When I lowered my hands to observe what happened, the upper part of the body of the man was dangling in front of me while his lower part was clearly on the roof. He appeared motionless. His face was bleeding profusely. I had pieces of glass in my mouth and hair and blood was covering my face, arms and clothes. I struggled to open the door that was blocked by the density of the crowd. Eventually I managed to get out, in a state of total shock. I was pushed and tossed by the masses of people, whose sole objective was to run and flee from a deadly threat, the nature of which none of them were aware.

Suddenly, I heard the scream of a man, who grabbed me violently by the arm uttering the words: 'Do you want to get lynched?' To this day, I have no idea how this person managed to see me, let alone to reach me. He pushed me into a car with two other persons. They were all Europeans. We sped off towards Oyster Bay on the other side of town. The city centre was empty except for some soldiers. We were accompanied by sporadic gunfire all along the route.

I was clearly dazed and oblivious to what was happening. I recall that my rescuer repeatedly asked me about my address. Apparently, I had no memory of anything at the time. The only response I had was to repeat the name George Rockey. Fortunately, the person knew George and took me to his residence. A dramatic scene ensued when George opened his front door and saw me standing there. He literally collapsed and passed out. At that moment, I thought it was my ghastly sight with blood covering all parts of my face and body that had caused that effect on George. Miriam told me they thought they were seeing a ghost. Apparently, word had circulated that I had been lynched by the crowd. My car had been found with the engine running. It was smashed and had blood all over it, both inside and on the outside and that there was no sign of 'me or my body'. In the midst of this scene of utter chaos, my rescuers left unnoticed. Clearly, they were anxious to rejoin their families. I did not have the presence of mind to thank them or ask for their names.

That night I stayed at the Rockeys. With the passing of each hour, I felt more tired physically and mentally. George and Miriam nursed me and were comforting me all the time in response to my repeated remark that I had killed a man. My only recollection the following morning was being in the car heading towards town. There was a total blank in my memory from that moment until I woke up at the Rockeys. I had fallen asleep with my clothes on. I had strong aches and pains all over my body, as if a steamroller had gone over me. I struggled to find enough energy to get to the bathroom. The sight of my face in the mirror littered with cuts and the blood all over me was stupefying.

It was painful to wash my face and I still had crystals of glass in the mop of hair on my head. Coming to the sitting room, I could hear the sound of the radio and saw the Rockey couple glued to it. Both rushed to escort me to an armchair with comforting words that all was well.

I had lost all sense of time and orientation. George told me that a mutiny had occurred and that British troops were called upon to squash it. He tried to reassure me that Nyerere was safe and mentioned that Kambona was trying to 'defuse' the situation. Several times, I asked what had happened to me and both ignored my remarks and continued to talk about the mutiny. It was only on the third day of us being housebound by the curfew imposed by the army that I regained a certain degree of normality, both physically and mentally.

Sensing my total loss of memory about what had happened, George told me I had a car accident but nothing serious had occurred. It took several weeks after the end of the mutiny before life in Dar began to return to normal. It was a very small community and everyone knew what had happened to me, yet not one single person murmured a word within my earshot.

When I went to see my car that had been towed to police headquarters, the chief of Dar's police Mr Singh, who was a friend, was exceptionally reserved in answering my questions. Equally surprising was that he did not pose a single question to me. His only concern was for me to take the car to a garage soonest, as its sight was 'reminiscent' of the mutiny days. It took me nearly five months to start regaining my memory about the accident.

The mystery was that when the police recuperated my car, there was no body on it. Also no death had been reported in connection with a car accident. The South African man who rescued me never identified himself.

George had no clue as to who he was. I placed several advertisements in the local papers requesting him to contact me, to no avail.

It was my fate and destiny to reach the brink of perishing and to miraculously survive. I always felt that the spirit and blessing of my father was both a driving and protecting force for me. I should mention that I only recounted the aforementioned experiences to my father several years later when we met after our long separation.

Rift in national leadership

The mutiny that was squashed within days marked the beginning of a new era in Tanzania. The solidarity of the one-party system TANU gave way to ideological differences between Nyerere and Kambona, the former with his socialistic inclination and the latter with his support for capitalism. The rift between the two leaders filtered through the ranks, creating an environment of rivalry and distrust. The changing political environment left in its wake major changes at all levels of the government and TANU.

Its impact on my work and working conditions became more evident with each passing week. Joeli and James, who were my counterparts, were rapidly losing their status of power, as they were looked upon as Kambona's protégés. The process of their phasing out was evident, though gradual. For my part, my relationship with Nyerere and Kambona remained unchanged. I was advised by George to restrict my contact with Kambona to responding to initiatives made by him.

One day I received a call informing me that Kambona wished to see me that night at his home. I was in no position to refuse. However, I informed George who advised me to be very cautious in every word I said. As customary, I was met very warmly by Kambona at the front door. Joeli was with him as well as two other persons I had never met before.

After a few minutes of talking about almost everything in general, he came to the object. Pointing to one of the two persons, Kambona told me that he was a journalist from Malawi and that he wanted to appoint him as news editor. He wanted me to gradually take over from James as editor-in-chief, while Joeli would retain his political overview of the operation. My response was brief and to the point. I told him he was the boss and it was him who decided on all such matters.

Kambona insisted that I stay for dinner and was visibly irritated when I politely declined. I had intended to go straight to George's home but decided to go to my place first as a precaution in the event that I was being followed. My memory of that evening remains extremely vivid. I sat in the armchair in the sitting room, with Kim the dog doing his customary Zulu dance around me to express his joy at my return.

It was then that it dawned upon me, without any doubt, that my days in Tanzania were numbered. Clearly, I was becoming embroiled in the political tug of war, a situation that could have extremely serious negative consequences on my welfare. Evidently, Kambona wished to tighten his grip on the official media. He was clearly aware that Joeli and James were being targeted by Nyerere's supporters and that their days were numbered.

Later in the evening, I went to see George and to report to him what had happened. To my surprise and amazement, he already had knowledge of what had ensued, which confirmed my fears that the conflict between Nyerere and Kambona had assumed a greater level of intensity and pro-portion. In fact, George informed me that the person Kambona proposed to replace me with was a member of his extended family that lived in Malawi. My succession to the post of joint editor-in-chief was a critical decision that would have far-reaching ramifications.

It was on that same unforgettable evening that George informed me, to my utter shock and dismay, that he had been diagnosed with cancer in both lungs. He intimated that he had already requested Nyerere to post him at the Embassy in London where he could get proper medical treatment.

I returned home in a state of bewilderment and despondency. The events of that day weighed heavily on me both mentally and physically, resulting in my dropping off to sleep on the couch in the sitting room. I recall being woken up next morning by the houseboy whose facial expres-sion reflected his shock at discovering me in this state and, more impor-tantly, to note that the front door had been left wide open.

I spent the entire morning at home analysing the events and situation. I thought of my father and wondered what advice he would give me in the face of these complex developments. The mere thought of him gave me considerable moral strength and a feeling that I would somehow sur-mount the crises. I had arranged to have lunch with George in town but he contacted me to say it was 'preferable' to meet at his home. George asked what my plans were for the future. My response was immediate and to the point. I told him I was resigning and leaving the country soonest. 'Young man, I hate to say it but you have taken the right and wise decision' was his resounding response. We spent the whole afternoon discussing the manner and procedure in which I should tender my resignation. He advised me to take the approach of having fulfilled my task dutifully and my earnest desire to seek a change in my career.

The ensuing week was one of the most memorable in my life. It had taken me nearly five years to establish and concretize my career in Tanzania. Dar had become my home and adopted country. The successive events and changes in the political environment as well as that of my professional status threatened to destroy everything that I had achieved. My dilemma was further confounded by the total insecurity for my future. My only option would be to return to the Middle East where I would be confronted by the negative mood that was prevalent towards anybody of Palestinian origin. Admittedly, I had enjoyed good wages in Dar but to live comfortably one was unable to make any substantial savings. Hence, the prospects for a change became more complex. I saw my world crumbling before me. The feeling of almost total impotence shrouded my days and nights. Somehow being a Palestinian refugee was a nightmare that remained to haunt one's life. With the exception of Jordan, where I was a national, all Arab countries would treat me in accordance with my place of birth – Palestine – and that was a taboo when it came to entry visas, let alone work permits.

Another door opens

One thing was clear: my decision to resign and leave the country, soonest, was irreversible. I had prepared the letter of resignation and discussed its contents with George. The evening of that day, I was sitting at home trying to work out some logistics vis-à-vis how best to approach Kambona, when the phone rang. The person on the other end of the line introduced himself as Mr Paul Khayat from Lebanon. He said he was visiting Dar for a couple of days and wished to meet with me. We agreed to meet next day for a drink at the New Africa Hotel, where he was staying. Putting down the phone, I well remember thinking that I had perhaps made an error by accepting that we meet without verifying the purpose.

The following day, I was submerged by work and it was only by chance that I recalled my appointment with Paul at the last minute. I went over to the hotel to see him. He was a fairly short man, immaculately dressed with an extremely warm and friendly disposition. He explained that he had a book publishing company in Beirut and that he had come to look for business prospects in Tanzania. Several officials in the government and private sector had spoken to him about me and he wished to know if I was interested in representing his business in East Africa. He spent a long time speaking in detail about his company's multiple operations and plans for expansion internationally. I was concentrating less on his remarks and more on whether or not I should tell him I was soon leaving Tanzania.

Knowing that he was returning to Beirut early the next morning, I decided to disclose to him my plans to resign. I did so in order to cut short the discussion and politely terminate the meeting. To my utter surprise, his immediate and spontaneous response was that he was ready and willing to offer me a job with his company in Beirut, with immediate effect. My reaction was one of disbelief. I questioned the seriousness of his offer, considering he hardly knew anything about me and my qualifications and experience. Paul was adamant that his offer was valid and authentic. He said he would make a draft of an agreement for employment containing the key elements and leave it for me next morning with the receptionist. The meeting ended with assurances on his part that I would be recruited upon arrival in Beirut, coupled with several embraces and a stream of compliments about my impressive personality and my achievements in Dar.

Shortly after I returned home, Paul phoned, though it was close to midnight, to tell me he had given the receptionist an envelope containing the offer for me. He said he hoped to see me in Beirut within a month or two at the latest. I was baffled and bewildered by that encounter. Could Paul be yet another proof to reconsolidate my belief in fate and destiny?

The next morning, on my way to work, I passed by the hotel and collected the letter from Paul with the offer. In fact, it was merely a paper with handwritten remarks stating a salary and some expenses. I was certainly not reassured by the presentation. However, I thought I would lose nothing to follow up on it in Beirut.

My main concern that day related to my letter of resignation. I had requested an appointment with Kambona and it was scheduled for the afternoon at his home. I had not met him or spoken to him since our last encounter when I had declined his invitation for dinner. During this interim period, his relative had taken up the post of news editor, while I assumed my responsibility as joint editor-in-chief. To my surprise, neither Joeli nor James ever discussed the change with me. Their attitude was one of being oblivious to the event, though it had a direct effect on their work and status.

Kambona was not at home at the time of our appointment, yet his security assured me that he was on his way. It was almost an hour later that he arrived, greeting me in a very friendly and apologetic manner. He asked me how his relative was progressing with his work and whether, in my opinion, he had the qualities and ability to become editor instead of James in the near future. He said James wanted to return to Ghana. He further divulged that Joeli was going to be replaced soon so he could devote more time to TANU affairs.

The revelations confirmed the urgent need for me to leave, yet made the timing of my resignation less opportune and more sensitive. For a moment, I thought I should postpone raising the issue of my resignation. However, when Kambona asked what I wished to discuss with him, I immediately responded that I wished to be relieved of my responsibilities as soon as possible. He did not seem to be in the least surprised. He listened very attentively to my explanation and reasons for resigning. When I handed the letter to him, he took some time to read it. He then put it on the table in front of him while a broad smile covered his face.

A deafening silence prevailed and though it lasted only for seconds, it felt like minutes. He told me that he had personally chosen me for the post because I was a man of 'principles and integrity'. He said Nyerere wanted to appoint Frene, who was not particularly enthusiastic about the job, as her priority at the time was the ANC and combating apartheid. He spoke at length about the 'admirable' manner in which I conducted my work and dealt with criticism by some politicians and members of TANU. He concluded by thanking me for my outstanding achievements in the service of the national media in Tanzania.

Before I could react to his remarks, Kambona told me that he was expecting my resignation and that he was aware of the real reasons for it. I must admit, I was utterly flabbergasted when he said that he fully understood my desire not to be mangled by the ongoing internal political conflict within TANU. He then asked when I intended to leave, adding that if

I wished to depart earlier than my stipulated three months' notice period, he would arrange for that. Our meeting ended on that note. While bidding me farewell at his front door, he gave me a paper containing his personal telephone number, telling me to call if I needed anything. To my surprise, he appeared quite emotional. He hugged me while repeatedly expressing thanks for what I had done for his country.

That was the last time I had personal contact with Kambona. He had, however, arranged to facilitate all formalities pertaining to my departure, which took place within six weeks. The future proved me right in the decision to leave when I did. It was just over one year later, in 1967, that Kambona together with his wife and children went into 'self-imposed' exile in the United Kingdom, claiming that his life was in danger, while Nyerere accused him of betrayal. From his sanctuary in London, Kambona became a bitter critic and opponent of Nyerere and his policies. In 1992, after living 25 years in exile, Kambona returned to Tanzania after it adopted multi-party democracy. He and the government became engaged in vilifying one another. The man who was a luminary in Tanzanian politics had lost his glamour and his following and was unable to regain his political status and clout. He died in London in 1997.

My departure from Dar es Salaam was a sad moment in my life. I was leaving my recently adopted country to venture into the unknown. I had developed friendships with a large cross-section of people of all nationalities, cultures and creeds. I loved Tanzania and genuinely felt part of its fabric. Reflecting on what happened, in retrospect what I considered as a premature departure was in fact both timely and opportune. My mission was accomplished. I needed to face the challenges of the outside world as a Jordanian born in Palestine, with all the implications that such a status constituted in the 'Arab' world.

5

Return to the Middle East

A Taste of What is to Come

It was prior to my departure from Dar es Salaam that I encountered an experience that was indicative of what awaited me. I had planned to make Cairo my first stop, to have the long-awaited reunion with my father. Egypt had maintained its prohibition of work for people of Palestinian origin, with or without pay, during my sojourn in East Africa. Hence, my intention was then to proceed to Lebanon to seek employment and to follow upon the offer made to me by Paul Khayat. Obtaining employment in Lebanon for a person of Palestinian origin, irrespective of his current nationality, was extremely difficult but not impossible. The process required the appropriate contacts, combined with financial offerings to key officials responsible for issuing work permits.

I had applied for a tourist visa for Egypt through its embassy in Dar. The Ambassador, Mr El-Essawi, a former high-ranking army officer whom I knew quite well, politely and diplomatically explained to me that he had to obtain approval from Cairo. There was no response for two weeks, much to the embarrassment of the Ambassador. I eventually had to change my plans and fly to Beirut, where a well-connected member of my family managed to obtain for me a tourist visa that would be granted upon arrival at Beirut airport. Proof of that had to be provided prior to my departure to the Tanzanian authorities and the airline company.

The positive side of that unexpected obstacle was that I was able to take Kim the dog with me on the same flight. The cost of his transportation was more expensive than mine and it was foreseen he would have to stay in quarantine at Beirut for a whole month. I was determined not to part company with my dog, irrespective of cost and the counselling of friends and family members, who considered my decision to lack all sense.

My journey from Dar to Beirut, in November 1966, is particularly vivid in my memory. My mind and body were charged by tense emotions for what I had left behind and what was awaiting me. During the long flight, I was not able to sleep for a single moment. The scene of my departure was omnipresent in my mind, compiled with snapshots of images of people and events of my East African years. Equally prevalent were visions and thoughts of what awaited me on arrival. A firm believer in fate and destiny, I was neither worried nor afraid of the unknown. More importantly, I had the will and determination to succeed in my new environment both professionally and socially.

I wondered what my sisters, who were then residing in Lebanon, would look like as well as other members of my family, uncles and cousins. In fact, it was at that moment I realized that the extended family that had taken up residence in Lebanon had considerably increased in number. The one thought that was permanent in my mind, however, was that of the arrival of my father within days and the moment of happiness of our anticipated reunion.

Arrival in Beirut

The scene at Beirut airport was one of joy and pleasure for the two dozen members of the family spearheaded by my sisters. In contrast to my life in Dar, a feeling of family belonging dawned on me. It was at that moment I realized that the years spent in Dar had been a world apart from any member of my family. Retrieving that feeling brought great comfort to me.

It took a few days before the celebrations and festive environment simmered down and I was able to start attending to my personal affairs. My first contact was with Paul Khayat. He was extremely welcoming. I was astounded by the luxury of his huge office premises and the large number of staff, well attired and enjoying spacious areas to accommodate their ultra-modern desks and most up-to-date equipment. His secretary, a Franco-Lebanese fashion model type, escorted me to Paul, who greeted me with an embrace and warm expressions of welcome.

He very proudly took me on a tour of his two-storey premises, introducing me to all staff we encountered. He and his elder brother Samir had expanded the family business, originally a bookshop, to a publishing company. The bookshop remained as their anchor, and was being run by the mother. His brother established a parallel business, selling property in Florida, USA, while Paul took charge of the publishing side.

During the ensuing few days, we discussed my job offer in detail and I was made to understand that what Paul had in mind for me was a public relations post. He already had an editor, an Englishman with considerable experience. He wished me to negotiate obtaining representation of international publishers as well as promoting the sales of his own publications. It was important and necessary for me to start work soonest, considering my residence status and financial situation. Hence, I accepted his offer and began working within a week.

I managed to rent a beautiful apartment in an excellent location for a reasonable amount, within walking distance to the office. Kim, the dog, shared the flat with me and matters were progressing on all fronts. Most important, the long-awaited arrival of my father from Cairo finally materialized. Without doubt, one of the happiest moments of my life was when my father emerged from the crowded arrivals at the airport. For years, I had dreamed and yearned for that moment. There was so much to recount on both sides, yet somehow we were initially content with simply savouring the ecstasy of our reunion by frequent warm embraces and exchanging looks of endearment. That night, my father showed more interest in my present and future plans rather than in my experience in Africa. I well understood his reaction. He wanted assurance that I had a job and a work permit. He was delighted to know about my employment with the Khayats but expressed deep concern: what if my work permit was refused? I went out of my way to dispel his fears in this regard, while knowing too well the pertinence of the issue he evoked.

It was only on that occasion that my father informed me about his own situation. He had personal relations with the late King Abdullah I of Jordan, initiated while he and the family were still in Palestine. My father also had good relations with a large number of Palestinians who had fled to Jordan, obtained the nationality and assumed key positions both in government and the private sector. It was through this network of high-level contacts that my father had obtained the Jordanian nationality for the family without actually being a resident of the country at that time.

Apparently, King Abdullah I offered my father a role as one of his personal advisers at the Royal Court and arrangements were in process to finalize his appointment. It was weeks before my father was to take up his post that the King was assassinated in Jerusalem and the project was abandoned. Following that, my father was offered several ministerial posts, some of which were of interest to him. However, my stepmother was adamant in not wanting to leave Egypt and equally so in her strong objection to residing in Jordan.

My father's professional prospects in Jordan were extremely rich and promising but were thwarted by the refusal of my stepmother to leave Egypt, though knowing that my father was prohibited to work in that country. In recounting these developments to me, my father blamed only himself for succumbing to the wishes of my stepmother. He did not want to fragment the family that was already victim to imposed separation and having to endure considerable problems as a consequence of the diaspora. Eventually, my father was appointed as Counsellor representing Jordan at the Arab League in Cairo, a post that secured his residence in Egypt but, ironically, put an end to his professional ambitions.

My father departed after ten days, during which we had a memorable get-together, the images of which remain vivid in my mind to this day. Having told him about my life and experience in East Africa, I sensed his pride and appreciation for what I had gone through and achieved. I believe it was at that juncture that, at the age of 30, I had earned his full confidence and respect as a self-reliant man.

It was in the early part of January 1967 that Paul wanted to see me urgently in his office. He announced to me that the request for my work permit was rejected. He proposed I meet his lawyer who was also a prominent journalist by the name of BJ. I was made to understand by BJ that I could obtain the permit provided that we make some arrangements with the key people responsible for issuing permits at the Ministry of Labour.

BJ arranged our visit to the Ministry and left, and in less than one hour I was in possession of my work permit. I recall leaving the Ministry with a feeling mixed of immense joy and anxiety. I could imagine the drastic consequences on my life and future without BJ as a contact.

At that time, Lebanon was enjoying a boom. Beirut was the pulsating heart of the Middle East capitals and living in that city was considered a privilege. For me what mattered most was that I was reunited with my sisters, that I had a residence permit for one year and that it was a good location for job-hunting in the region. It was clear that if I did not capitalize on my stay in Lebanon to obtain a job with better financial and professional prospects, my future would be in peril. With each passing month, I became more aware that with all the pomp and luxury of my work environment, and the kindness of Paul, my job did not relate to my qualifications or experience or my professional aspirations.

My sister Pakiza worked for the United Nations Relief and Works Agency for Palestine Refugees in the Near East (UNRWA), while Farihan had a job as a secretary at the British Embassy. Hence, both were secure vis-à-vis their residence in the country. They shared a flat and had developed a network of friends. They were happy and content with their working and social environments, a situation that brought much relief and satisfaction to me. An added consolation was that they had maternal uncles, aunts and cousins residing in the neighbourhood with whom they were in regular contact.

Again fate and destiny had it that a friend of my sister Farihan by the name of Raja Hanoush worked for a leading head-hunting company in Lebanon. I had met Raja, who was of Palestinian origin, at my sister's home one evening. He had been invited to dinner with his sister who was a close friend of Pakiza and Farihan. During the course of the evening, Raja and I exchanged information about each other's professional history. He expressed interest in my journalistic credentials and inquired whether I would be interested in a posting in one of the Gulf States. The evening ended with agreement that I would provide my CV to Raja in the hope of possible job opportunities.

Before three months had elapsed, Raja phoned to inform me of a vacancy for a post of Press Officer with the Kuwait Oil Company. He asked if I would be interested, while emphasizing that there were other candidates and that the process of selection would require some time. It would also involve written exams and a series of interviews for the candidates.

The Kuwait Oil Company beckons

The prospects of working in Kuwait appealed very much to me. That country had become the refuge for Palestinians to obtain white-collar jobs. It was going through a considerable development process sparked by its expanding oil and gas industries. The Kuwait Oil Company (KOC) was a large employer of Palestinians. Its headquarters was in Al Ahmadi, a self-contained and sustained city, where all the employees resided. It was a beautifully planned city with bungalows and gardens for the senior staff and small, one-storey apartments for the junior staff and single staff. It had its own hospital, shopping mall, social clubs and cinemas. There were police and immigration offices that dealt specifically with the affairs of the residents. In fact, living in Al Ahmadi was a different lifestyle, more free and liberal than any other part of the country. For policy reasons, the official office premises of the KOC managing director were in Kuwait city. They housed the chief executive, his assistant and a number of staff members. I knew all that because my cousin Aref had managed to get a job with KOC as translator and had been living there for several years with his mother Mirvet and his wife Hind.

As my first year of residence in Lebanon was coming to an end nothing had concretized with regard to new job opportunities. Arrangements had already been made with BJ for our visit to the Ministry of Labour to have my permit renewed under the same conditions.

What alarmed me most was that Khayat's was facing serious financial problems. Apparently, Paul's flamboyant management style coupled with his desire to expand operations too rapidly placed the company in peril of bankruptcy. It was through a cousin of mine, who was manager of a leading American bank in Beirut, that I learned about Khayat's financial crises, which Paul had succeeded in keeping a well-guarded secret. My permit was renewed for another year and so was my contract with Khayat's, in spite of the company's financial problems. Nevertheless, concern over my future became a main preoccupation for me.

Two major events occurred during the months that followed. The first was that I met my future wife Christianne, who was visiting Lebanon to meet local friends, whom she got to know while her father was serving in Beirut as a French Foreign Ministry official.

The second was that I had at last received a communication from KOC that I had been short-listed for the post of Press Officer. I was requested to be in Kuwait within two weeks for written tests and interviews that would last for a week. While I was ready to accept almost any job at that time, the idea of working for KOC was especially appealing and exciting to me. I had already been warned by Raja that the tests and interviews would be 'tough and intensive'. I had no indication whatsoever about the type or nature of exams I would be subjected to. The only preparation I could do was to acquaint myself with the structure and operations of KOC as well as with the history of the State of Kuwait.

My arrival in Kuwait marked a new era in my life. I was determined to succeed in getting the job with KOC. Besides the importance of and excitement about the test and interviews awaiting me, I was looking forward to the pleasure of meeting my cousin Aref, his mother and family as well as Nermin, my cousin for whom Aref succeeded in obtaining a secretarial job with KOC.

Leaving my luggage at the guesthouse, I was immediately taken by Aref to his house where I passed the evening with the family members. Both Aref and my aunt were very well connected with the Al Ahmadi community. Aref was an exemplary official, who was liked and respected for his friendly character. He was an athlete who was champion of the tennis and squash rackets tournaments for several consecutive years. My aunt, Mirvat, was a social dynamo whose residence was the meeting place for most wives and their children. She was renowned for her exquisite oriental cooking and for the almost daily sessions of games of cards, particularly that of 'quatorze'.

A good part of the evening was spent talking about the working and living conditions at KOC. It was evident that KOC offered all I needed at that juncture of my life with regard to career development and job security. I learned that Aref and my aunt were friendly with Kamal Ali, the head of the department that I would be working for. However, he was not concerned with the examination process, which was entirely handled by George Selhab, who would be the direct chief of the selected candidate. Apparently, George was extremely strict and rigid in his work.

I can never forget my first night at the guest house. I was charged with emotions of both anxiety and joy. Though I was confident of my professional abilities, getting that job became a prime objective for me. The thought of returning to Beirut empty-handed was a nightmare scenario, which I tried to eliminate from my thoughts. The idea of becoming a KOC official grew on me so rapidly and intensely that it became a motivation and inspiration.

Interviews at KOC

I arrived at the Press and Public Information Department a few minutes before eight in the morning. On entering the office premises, I was struck by the simple yet spotless vision that confronted me. I was escorted by a secretary to a waiting room and was informed that my first meeting would be with George Selhab. Within minutes, I was facing George who was friendly but never smiling. He informed me that the two other short-listed candidates, an Egyptian and an Iraqi, had already been tested and interviewed.

He handed to me the programme of my five-day stay and we went through it item by item during which time he provided me with some clarifications and additional information. George made it clear that the post was for an assistant to him, that he was the person to determine the choice of the successful candidate and that dedication and loyalty were a key criteria for the job.

On average, I spent half a day on written tests and the other half on interviews. My last but one interview was with the Director of Human Resources, Alan Horan, who was an Old Victorian. His parents, who were British, lived in Alexandria for many years, during which he was schooled at Victoria College.

My final interview was with Kamal Ali, who intimated to me that I was selected for the job while underlining that the news would be transmitted to me officially by George and that I should pretend ignorance until he made the announcement to me. Though overwhelmed with joy, I struggled to contain myself until meeting George.

The picture of that late afternoon encounter is still vivid in my mind. When I entered George's office, he greeted me with a smile, gesturing for me to take a seat. He congratulated me on the 'excellent' exams I had done and informed me that he had decided to appoint me for the post in question.

The minute I went out of the building, I screamed out loud with joy. I looked up to the sky, thanking God for his support and for realizing my dream. Within minutes, I was on the phone to my father who was delighted with the news.

It was an evening of celebration with my aunt and the family. Somehow, it was at that moment that I felt a sense of normality returning to my existence as a human being. No longer did I need fear being branded as a Palestinian in obtaining a job or residence. Finally, I had an opportunity to construct a normal and stable life, to develop my professional career and, equally important, to plan for the future.

Returning to Beirut was a historic event. My outlook and attitude towards everything had changed drastically. I was totally liberated from all worries and anxieties relating to life in Lebanon. Paul was pleased with the news of my imminent departure and the positive prospects awaiting me.

Somehow, what at times was a hostile environment for me became a friendly and even welcoming one. My official status was transformed into a welcomed visitor for whom doors were always open and attitudes positive and hospitable.

I was scheduled to commence work with KOC within three months. I was swamped by the deluge of arrangements and preparations that needed to be finalized prior to my departure. The most important, and much to my regret to this day, concerned finding a 'good home' for Kim, the dog. Kuwait was not at all the place to own a dog at the time and I was officially discouraged by Alan Horan from bringing Kim with me to Al Ahmadi.

My contract stipulated a three-month probation period and I was determined not to allow any element to threaten the continuity of what was a golden chance for me to secure my future.

6

Kuwait

A Major Change in my Life

The five years I spent in Kuwait were undoubtedly the most challenging and important in my career. It was clear from the outset that my move to Kuwait gave me the opportunity to construct a more stable and solid professional and personal life. At long last, I managed to achieve a sense of security. I was accepted as a member of the KOC community with all that this entailed: a regular income with many fringe benefits and a working environment that was of the highest standard. Much to my disappointment, these conditions were to change considerably due to unforeseen circumstances that KOC was subjected to.

Al Ahmadi was in a way a perfect refuge for people of many nationalities, who opted to go to that small developing state in the desert, to escape the political turmoil and social instability that plagued many of the Arab countries at the time.

There were two categories of people. One included those who decided to make Al Ahmadi the long-term residence and home for them and their family members. The other comprised those who used Al Ahmadi as a stopgap for their career development, with the intention of seeking their good fortunes elsewhere whenever the appropriate opportunity arose.

At the outset, I certainly was among the first category. Al Ahmadi was the answer to my dream. It provided me with all the assurances and security that I had longed for since my departure from Palestine. I remember well my cousin Aref and my aunt who considered Al Ahmadi as their new-found country. Their future was deeply embedded in Al Ahmadi, where they enjoyed a 'normal' life.

Fate and destiny were again omnipresent factors in the years I spent in Kuwait. In retrospect, I realize how one's plans and life could be altered drastically by unexpected, unforeseen events.

Growth in family and work

Before I delve into the substance of my Kuwaiti experience, let me state joyfully that I got married before I signed my contract with KOC. My wife Christianne (Tina) was to join me after the probation period. However, I was warned from the outset that it might take several more months for married accommodation to be allocated. In reality, the delay was considerable and as a consequence, my eldest daughter Aida was born in Beirut. Eventually mother and daughter arrived in Al Ahmadi and we were installed in a lovely two-bedroom bungalow that became my first home since departing from Palestine in 1948.

By that time, I had been confirmed with an open-ended contract and my career development was shaping up in a positive manner. Within a year, I had consolidated my position in the Public Information Department to the extent that a sizeable amount of George's responsibilities were gradually transferred to me. At the outset, George openly expressed dissatisfaction but he soon succumbed to the decisions of his superiors. It was only later that I came to know that the timing of these changes coincided with George's plans for retirement. I learned also that KOC was starting a process of 'Kuwaitization' and secret plans were in the making to 'contract out' or 'privatize' all that was considered as non-essential services such as our department.

One morning, Kamal Ali informed me that a decision was taken for me to be stationed at the Office of the General Manager, Mr Rallston, in Kuwait City. My duties and responsibilities would remain unchanged. The only addition was that I would give a verbal briefing to Rallston every morning on news published by the local media on KOC. As of that day, my status with KOC assumed a new dimension and it became apparent that I was being groomed for other future tasks.

My new posting privileged me to have a plush executive office and, more importantly, to mingle on a daily basis with Rallston and Mr Ahmed Hijazi, the legal adviser of KOC. These privileges, however, claimed their price with regard to the pressure of my work and the extremely long working hours. Invariably, I would be called upon to perform tasks at night and very frequently on weekends. It was an environment that motivated me and made me excel in all aspects of my work. I loved my work and revelled in the sense of achievement almost on a daily basis.

An added joy to my life was the arrival of my second daughter, Karima, who was born in the Ahmadi Hospital in September 1970.

Restructuring at KOC

While everything in my life was progressing well, during my second year at KOC, rumours were constantly circulated about imminent changes in the structure of the company. It was early in 1971 that the contracting out of all non-essential services was officially announced. This entailed the transfer and termination of all staff who worked in the concerned departments, including the Public Information Department. The most troubling aspect was that it was envisaged that 25 per cent of the workforce would be relinquished in the process. Though some mention had been made occasionally about such a measure, no one expected it to happen so soon or that it would be conducted in one single stage.

The news had a bombshell effect at KOC. The hundreds of officials affected by the changes, including me, were in shock. How well I recall my feeling of betrayal on the part of KOC: I had put all my heart, energy and dedication into my work, only now to be abandoned to roam in the orbit of insecurity and the unknown.

I could hardly wait for daybreak to go to the office. I was determined to ask Rallston to assist me in remaining with KOC, in whatever capacity. Al

Ahmadi had provided me with my long-awaited refuge where I began to construct a new home, life and future. I was neither willing nor prepared to lose all those factors at that juncture.

Waiting to meet Rallston was an endless torture. When his secretary eventually came in person to inform me he was ready to see me, I was suddenly possessed by an unexplainable sense of confidence and strength. I was ready and prepared for the worst-case scenario. Entering his immense office, I noted that Rallston had already positioned himself in the sitting area away from his desk. He met me with a friendly smile and asked me to sit on the couch. He opened the conversation by telling me that my job was guaranteed with the contractor and that I would be running the entire operation.

Our department had been contracted out to an enterprise by the name of Mass Consultants and Services that had been established very recently for that purpose. The company was owned by Sheikh Mishaal, a high-ranking member of the ruling family, and a very senior official of the Ministry of Petroleum, Mr Abdul Karim Shawa, a naturalized Kuwaiti of Palestinian origin. Mass would provide KOC with services identical to those performed by the liquidated department. It would be remunerated every quarter in advance. George was retiring. Kamal Ali, the sole person to be retained by KOC, would be responsible for the overall supervision of the operation. I would be appointed Deputy General Manager of Mass and would be responsible for all aspects of its functioning. However, Mr Rallston diplomatically intimated that the post of General Manager would be held by a non-Arab for 'policy reasons'. He went out of his way to explain that this person would be a figurehead.

He portrayed the change as a positive development for my career, adding that the KOC contract with Mass stipulated my recruitment as a condition. I would be offered the same salary but would have to negotiate other conditions with Mass. Rallston explained that KOC would allow me to retain my residence in Al Ahmadi for up to three months to enable me to find accommodation in Kuwait City, where Mass would be located. It became clear that KOC's interest was that I should accept the change. It would have been naive and futile on my part to resist or attempt to change the decision.

Returning to my office, my mind suddenly drifted all the way back to my childhood in Jerusalem. How happy I was there! I went through snapshots of people and events at that juncture of my life, then drifting into the sequence of my life in Egypt, the UK, Africa and Lebanon. The question that loomed in my mind was, 'Will I and my family ever have a real home, a normal and stable life or will the diaspora haunt us forever after?'

Again fate and destiny caused a dramatic and major change in my life at a time when I had resigned myself to building a future with KOC. Or was it more my acceptance of fate and destiny? Suddenly, as though I had woken up from a nightmare, the positive side of the events dawned upon me. I could have been among those who were being terminated and had no job offer from the contractor. I had learned in my life to appreciate whatever I had and it was at that moment that the words of my father at the early stage of my career rang loud in my ears. 'Be ambitious and aim at the furthest star but always look back and see the many who are less fortunate than you.' At that moment, the secretary appeared at the door of my office and questioned why I was smiling. My response, which puzzled her, was that I was at the dawn of my new career.

Within two months, my family and I had settled into a semi-detached villa in a residential area called Salmiya. Our office premises were located on the fourth floor of a building in the centre of Kuwait City. My contractual conditions lacked considerable benefits, which I had with KOC.

I soon found out that our manpower had been reduced by one-third and that we were expected to generate and handle other contracts. AS, who was the active partner of Mass, made it clear from the outset that staff who did not justify their salaries would be terminated. I was informed that the managing director would not be appointed for at least two months and that I had to manage on my own. It was in this environment that I had to initiate and run the operations.

Challenges at Mass Consultants

Irrespective of all the problems and difficulties, I was determined to have the company succeed. The challenge became my force and motivation. To me, there was no option but to succeed. During the first two months,

KOC expressed its full satisfaction with the services Mass was providing to it. In addition, I had succeeded in finalizing substantive contracts with several other oil companies, including Aminoil and Getty. The volume of work had increased considerably and staff members were complaining about the conditions and the long working hours. Whenever I raised this subject with AS, he made it clear that Mass was not ready to engage additional staff in the foreseeable future. Needless to say, I was the main victim of the situation, having to work for extremely long hours and often on tasks entirely beyond my terms of reference. My moment of great joy was after six months, when AS informed me that the general manager had been recruited and would commence work within a week.

On arrival IK, a British national, was full of enthusiasm and energy. His last job had been with a public relations company in London where he enjoyed a good reputation. However, within six weeks, IK resigned and left Kuwait abruptly. It appeared that he and KOC and Mass did not see eye to eye on the major policy and management issues.

While urgent prospection was being made for a new general manager, it occurred to me to propose my friend and former colleague George Rockey. He had been working at the Tanzanian Embassy in London, while recuperating from a major lung operation. Destiny and fate would have it that George had written to me enquiring about job opportunities in Kuwait. So I submitted his CV to AS, who in turn gave it to KOC. After extensive interviews in London, George was offered the job. The reunion with George and his family in Kuwait was a memorable event in my life. Besides the joy of seeing him as well as Miriam, Timothy and 'Kim-the-Kim' (as opposed to 'Kim-the-dog'!), I had the enormous satisfaction of having been instrumental in helping him obtain this new job.

Always the superb professional, George lost no time in getting to grips with all aspects of the operation. Though his health was fairly fragile, he exerted considerable effort and time in handling the daily work and in building good relations with KOC.

As time went by, we became the victims of our own success. Business was expanding considerably while AS maintained a position of status quo vis-à-vis having additional staff.

Victims of our own success

One morning, as I was getting out of bed, I felt my heart pounding loudly at an exceptional high speed. My wife observed that something abnormal was happening to me and insisted that I go immediately to the doctor. The verdict was that I was on the verge of having a heart attack as a result of extreme exhaustion and stress. I was kept in hospital for three days under sedation and observation.

My father arrived the day I was admitted to hospital. He was extremely saddened by the event. His predicament was the acknowledgement that for me to obtain another job would be extremely difficult. Accordingly, his counsel was that I should work less while knowing that any change in the tempo would be short-lived. Within two weeks, my father returned to Cairo and life returned to its normal rhythm.

One positive factor resulting from my hospitalization was that AS spared me a considerable amount of arguments and tension that were habitual in the past. More importantly, my flirtation with the heart attack was an eye-opener to my precarious situation with regard to my career and future. My employment provided me with a good salary but nothing with regard to social security or pension. I decided to waste no time or effort in seeking a job that would provide me and my family with the basic needs that someone with my status must possess. Following considerable research, it became obvious that employment with the UN or one of its specialized organizations was my best option.

At the time, my sister Farihan had terminated her work with the British Embassy and had obtained the job of secretary to the Director of the International Labour Office (ILO) in Beirut. She enlightened me about working at the UN and was more than satisfied with the security and fringe benefits it offered. At the same time, she underlined the intense competition for jobs at the UN and the difficulties of being selected. All I could do at that stage was ask her to keep me informed about job vacancies that might correspond to my qualifications.

I resumed being immersed in my work, the volume of which expanded considerably due to the multiple additional contracts I obtained for Mass. It was a 'Catch-22' situation. My motivation and hard work generated additional responsibilities, which I had to perform myself. There was no way that

AS was going to recruit additional staff, irrespective of the volume of revenue. In effect, I was the victim of my own success. I was captive of a situation that appeared to have no solution but one: namely, to obtain another job.

Suddenly, unexpected events occurred at the business and family levels. George had a serious health relapse and was advised by a consortium of doctors to return immediately to the United Kingdom for urgent treatment. Within days, he and his family departed. That was indeed a dramatic and sad moment for me. A few months later, I received news from Miriam that he had passed away. Such tragedy, such sadness.

Within weeks of that loss, doctors at Ahmadi Hospital diagnosed my cousin Aref with a terminal disease. Within months, that six-foot athlete, radiating with energy and good health, also passed away. His wife Hind, together with the four children and my aunt, returned to Lebanon, her country of origin.

Despite my faith in fate and destiny, I found myself struggling to comprehend this dramatic sequence of events. It was an extremely difficult phase in my life. Yet I had a strong premonition that the tide would soon turn in my favour.

The ILO beckons

How well I remember that early morning when Farihan phoned to inform me that the ILO had announced a call for candidatures for a post of Regional Information Officer for the Arab States, to be based at its office in Cairo. Within days, I submitted my application to the ILO headquarters in Geneva. I was made to understand by Farihan that I should not expect to have any initial reaction for several months.

Nearly six months elapsed before I received a communication informing me that I had been short-listed. I was required to sit for written exams that would last for five days and a choice was given to me to undertake the tests either in Kuwait or Beirut, where the ILO had offices.

Quite naturally, I opted for Kuwait, as I could not officially absent myself from work. I was well aware that seeking job opportunities would be tantamount to an act of betrayal in the minds of my employers, and thus, these exams had to be conducted in a clandestine manner.

The five days proved to be among the most precarious in my life. Each day I would commence at nine in the morning until one in the afternoon. In the meantime, I had to juggle my work at Mass and ensure no break in delivery to our clients. Upon concluding my last test, my relief was beyond description. The exercise was demanding both in content and the time factor and I emerged with a feeling that whatever the outcome, I had performed to the best of my ability.

Weeks and months passed without any news from the ILO. I had resigned myself to the thought that nothing would materialize from that source and that I should begin seriously scouting for other job prospects. One morning, I had just arrived at my office when my direct telephone rang and the person at the other end announced himself as Chafik Sanadiki, the Director of the ILO Office in Kuwait. He informed me that I was required to go to the Organization's headquarters in Geneva within the week. I was to spend four days there, during which time I would have a series of interviews.

Interview in Geneva

My rejoicing at this news was impeded by the stress and the complex and cumbersome plans and arrangements I had to make to cover up for my departure abroad for one week. But I managed. By the time I arrived in Geneva, I had shed off all the fears and negative thoughts related to this tense week. I was captivated by the impressive building housing the ILO headquarters on the shore of Lake Geneva. Its grandiose halls and offices and majestic meeting rooms were reminiscent of the history of that organization established in 1919.

My first meeting was with John Western (JW), the Head of the Press Department, a pipe-smoking American, whose casual mannerism inspired an informal and friendly environment. He lost no time in telling me that the results of my tests were outstanding and that I had been selected to occupy the post. He explained that my interviews were routine and were intended primarily to meet the key people with whom I would have work relations. We spent the morning together and he was kind enough to invite me to lunch, after which he took me on a tour of the building. I was quite reassured by his positive remarks and by the fact that he was introducing me to all officials we encountered as the new Regional Press Officer for the Arab States. Returning to my hotel that evening, I was overwhelmed with joy and happiness. I recall telling myself things were too good to be true. Despite my eagerness to break the good news to my father and family in Kuwait, I had a strange notion to retain that announcement until I signed the contract.

My interviews during the following few days were with a number of senior officials, mainly in technical departments. JW was right in the sense that the interviews were to brief me on the way their departments functioned as a newcomer staff member rather than to evaluate me.

The last but one day was spent at the medical department where I had thorough tests to determine my health and physical condition. That day's programme ended with meeting JW. When I entered his office, as was his habit, he had his feet up on his desk, his legs stretched out. He signalled me to take a seat. He then brought out a bottle of bourbon and a couple of glasses from one of the drawers. His face lit up with a grand smile, as he told me that this was to celebrate my appointment and to welcome me to his department. Our encounter that evening was brief yet pleasant. As I was leaving his office, he told me I should report to Mr Getty (PG) in the Personnel Department at ten in the morning to sign my contract.

How well I recall that evening and my walk from that palatial building along the lake all the way to my hotel. I was so overwhelmed with happy emotions that I could hear the pounding of my accelerated heartbeat. I could imagine the reaction to the good news on the faces of my father and family. I also envisaged the reaction of my employers and entertained some anxiety about their possible retribution. It was at that moment that I asked myself why it was that I was never able to fully enjoy such happy moments of my life. With time, the answer to that question became evident and clear. It was the element of insecurity, the lack of belonging, the inability to have a fall-back as safe haven that is called home. That was a trait symptomatic to being a refugee. Thus, despite my compelling urge to break the good news to my family, I went through the anguish of restraining myself for fear that something could go amiss.

Next morning, I arrived at the office of PG ahead of the time and was in the corridor when I heard my name being called. It was PG who came towards me with warm friendly greetings. He was an Italian who had been with the ILO for many years and took pride in relating the history of his career. I took an immediate liking to this man, who demonstrated interest in his work and those with whom he made contact. He had my contract offer before him and began explaining to me the terms and conditions. We had been together for nearly half an hour when his telephone rang. His facial expression portrayed surprise and anxiety as he listened with great attention.

Putting down the receiver, he informed me it was JW on the phone to advise him that, regrettably, the financial resources of the post I was to occupy had been taken by decision of a Deputy Director-General to fund another post at the ILO Office in Cairo. Naturally, the processing of my contract ended at that juncture and I was asked to go to see JW.

I could never forget the scene I witnessed upon arrival at JW's office. The profuse puffing of his pipe had created a layer of heavy smoke in the room. He was screaming at the top of his voice that what had happened was totally unacceptable, that he had already asked for an urgent meeting with the concerned DDG and that unless the funds were returned, he would resign from his post. Seeing me at the door, he took me by the arm, telling his secretary we were going to have a chat over a cup of coffee in the cafeteria.

By the time we were seated, he had calmed down considerably. He asked whether PG had told me what had happened, to which I replied in the affirmative. He let out a stream of words of fury followed by an unexpected silence that lasted for over a minute. JW came back to reality. He calmly told me that he could do nothing about the 'inappropriate' decision taken by the DDG. He assured me that the post would be offered to me once funds were available, but that he could not place a time-frame for that to happen. We parted on that note.

Up to this day, when I think of that development in retrospect, I am unable to explain or understand my reaction at that time. I was not surprised by the sudden and unexpected turn in events. My reaction was one of deep disappointment but nothing beyond that. I had been looking forward so much to my posting in Cairo that would have reunited me with my father after the endless years of separation. This was my main regret. I was so gratified that my premonition prevented me from transmitting any positive information to my family earlier.

I spent the entire evening and a good part of that night thinking of what was to come upon my return to Kuwait. In a sense, I had resigned myself to the fact that my short- and medium-term dream for a change in my career had been washed away. What remained was probably the long term. Yet all that depended on what fate and destiny had in store for me.

Awaiting confirmation

Upon my return to Kuwait, I was swamped by work that had accumulated during my absence. In a way, that situation was a blessing as it gave me little or no time to reflect back on what had happened in Geneva. Ironically, AS was becoming far less frequent with his criticism of the operation and the working environment had become more agreeable and tolerable. Knowledge about my trip to Geneva was restricted to my wife, father and sisters. Its mention was taboo, fearing leakage of the information and possible reprisal by my employers. Such was the atmosphere in which we lived. The nightmare scenario was always to find oneself suddenly out of a job without financial or logistical support. Following several months, I picked up the will to begin prospecting for jobs anywhere other than Kuwait. Somehow, despite the comfortable life my family and I had and the amenities surrounding us, I saw no possible professional advancement for me.

Nearly a year had elapsed when I received a telephone call from Chafik Sanadiki (CS), the Director of the ILO Office in Kuwait, informing that he had an urgent and important letter for me from his headquarters. I had actually lost hope of employment with the ILO and had forgotten all about the Geneva episode. So this was a surprise to say the least.

When I entered his office that afternoon, CS was extremely welcoming. He handed over to me a large sealed envelope, the contents of which I soon discovered were known to him. CS told me that I was being offered the job that had been previously denied due to financial constraints. The thick envelope contained my contract and a stream of documents, which CS helped me understand. It was the month of July 1973 and I was to commence my work at the Cairo Office in the beginning of October.

In a state of semi-shock, I went directly home. I told my wife what had happened and then spent several hours going through the contract and other documents. My recruitment conditions were the same as those offered to me in Geneva nearly a year before. There would be a decrease in my present salary of nearly 30 per cent. I had all along been prepared to accept that, in view of the numerous fringe benefits and the pension scheme. In addition to that, the move to Cairo would realize my long-hoped for dream of being reunited with my father.

I spent a sleepless night. I was in a state of ecstasy and disbelief, wondering whether this time things would materialize. By the morning, I had decided to sign the contract and submit my resignation. By midday, I had given the signed contract to CS and proceeded to discuss arrangements regarding travel for my family and myself and the transport of personal effects. I had also prepared my letter of resignation to give to AS that evening.

Our encounter remains so vivid in my mind. I can never forget the expression of shock on his face while reading my letter. The expression then transformed into a broad smile. His immediate reaction was to offer me a substantial increase in pay and to recruit additional staff to relieve me from the pressure of work. I told him I needed to have a total change in the direction of my career, that I was joining the ILO and that my decision was final. At the end of our meeting, it was clear that AS thought he could induce me to change my mind. He proposed we meet the following day with his partner, Sheikh M, indicating that matters could be sorted out to my satisfaction.

That night, I decided to be courteous but firm at our anticipated meeting and not to permit matters to prolong. Next evening, the mood was more tense and charged with emotions. I was offered a considerable increase in salary and shares in the company. When I responded negatively, both men became visibly upset, saying my departure would be conditional to a three-month notice period and that I should find a qualified candidate to replace me.

It took me nearly two months of daily discussions and persuasion before they eventually had a change in attitude and accepted my departure. I was determined to leave on good terms. Though we had our differences, both Sheikh M and AS were men for whom I had the greatest respect and who considered me with much regard and appreciation.

As my family and I were ready to embark on a new life, fate and destiny would again prove that the most unexpected can suddenly occur to change all plans.

In October 1973, war broke out between Egypt and Israel, making it impossible for me to take up my post as anticipated. Fortunately, the conflict did not last for long and my family and I left Kuwait for Cairo early in November 1973.

7

The ILO

The Horizon of an International Career

I was so excited to start my career with the ILO that I became oblivious to the environment that awaited me in Cairo in the wake of the
war with Israel. Several months before the breakout of hostilities, my
father had joined my stepmother in the United States, where she had been
on a prolonged visit to her children residing there. Hence, I was ready
to arrive in the absence of my father, who had promised to return at the
earliest possible date. Arrangements had been made that we would reside
at my father's apartment in Heliopolis until such time as we found a flat
closer to my work place in Zamalek. Another disappointing factor was
the absence of my aunt Husnieh, who had gone to visit her daughter Nihal
in Saudi Arabia and had been caught up by the military events. Her husband Nassib was the only member of our close family to welcome us upon
arrival.

The mood in the country was sombre and tense. People were still
mourning the dead and the injured. All spoke of the horrors of the war
and the devastating social and economic conditions it left in its aftermath.

The ILO Office premises was an imposing three-storey villa in the prestigious district of Zamalek, formerly a residence of one of the privileged Egyptian families. The building was transformed to accommodate some 30 international and local staff members. The Director, Aziz Al-Maraghi, was an Egyptian who had had long relations with the ILO. His deputy was Syrian and, by strange coincidence, was succeeded a few months after my arrival by CS, the official who headed the ILO Office in Kuwait during my examination period.

As promised, my father arrived in Cairo during the last week of November 1973. Our reunion marked one of the happiest days in my life. At long last, I was able to enjoy his company and to compensate for the years of separation imposed by the splintering of the family, following our forced departure from Palestine in 1948. It was a dream come true. The pleasure and joy I had each morning on seeing him before going to work was complemented by the same feeling upon my return. Most evenings we would have dinner on the large balcony and watch the news on television. Afterwards, the ritual was to play 'trick track' or backgammon. Though he was the better player, occasionally I would win due to a stroke of luck. These were the times of the greatest joy, particularly when he moaned about his bad luck. He immensely enjoyed being with my family and regularly volunteered to do the shopping. Though Heliopolis had expanded considerably since we moved there in the early 1950s, our neighbourhood had maintained its community environment. Residents like my father were known and welcomed wherever they went. It was a life of bliss for me. I was happy on all fronts and looked forward to the future with unreserved optimism.

My father meets his Maker

On the last day of December 1973, tragedy struck. We had decided to celebrate the arrival of the New Year quietly at home. I challenged my father to a game of backgammon but he declined. He was not himself at all. When I asked if he was all right, he responded with a nod and a forced smile on his face. He did not wish to have dinner, saying he would probably go to bed early. It was around 11 o'clock when I heard him call my name from the bathroom. I went rushing and found him bent over the washbasin. To my shock and horror, I saw he had vomited blood. He was visibly shaken with a querying expression of bewilderment on his face. I managed to compose myself and assured him that everything would be all right. I was at a total loss. I knew no doctors. Hospitals and clinics were inundated by the war casualties and, to compound matters, it was New Year's Eve when even emergency services were scarce. Even at this age and stage of my life, I find it too painful and traumatizing to recount my dramatic experience of that night and the following day. My father passed away on New Year's Day of 1974. He was 73 years old; I was 37.

In the midst of that tragedy, a rude reminder of non-belonging was manifested in a problem that would have never arisen, had we remained in Palestine: that of where to bury my father. Certainly not in our family cemetery in Jerusalem, as that was prohibited by the Israeli authorities. The family had never lived in Jordan, so that was not a practical option. Cairo imposed itself as the only location, and my father was made to rest in peace in a communal cemetery for 'Palestinian Martyrs', a name that mystifies me to this day.

I was blessed to have an elderly relative, Mustafa Al-Taji, who literally handled all the endless and most cumbersome and complex formalities pertaining to a deceased person. His efficiency, kindness and support will forever remain dearly appreciated by me.

My sorrow was deepened by the thought of the historic funeral of my grandfather in Jerusalem and the extreme contrast to that of his son, whose death passed almost unnoticed except for a handful of immediate relatives and friends.

A sense of extreme frustration and anger occupied me for the weeks and months that followed. I was unable to digest the injustice of being deprived of our homeland and even more of having no right to be buried in our family cemetery next to our ancestors. Why my father was prohibited from resting in peace next to his father and my mother in Jerusalem is proof of the cruelty and injustice that unfortunately remains prevailing in our world of today.

Again, fate and destiny proved that the unexpected is a key factor in our life. My great consolation was that my father and I had spent the last month of his life together and that I was by his side when he passed away.

Having got over the initial shock of that devastating event, I sought refuge and a means of pacification by submerging myself in my job and new responsibilities. From the outset, it was clear that the nature of my work would require me to travel extensively in the Middle East and North Africa. Occupying a newly created post demanded that I set up a network of contacts with the media throughout these regions.

Al-Maraghi wanted to expand and enlarge the jurisdiction of his office that had responsibility for Egypt and Sudan. Accordingly, he welcomed me as an addition to his professional staff while expecting that my activities would enhance the standing and status of the office. Within months, I established good relations with key media and audio-visual figures in Cairo as well as most west Asian and North African countries.

The feedback on my work performance from Geneva was extremely positive. This development had a direct impact on Al-Maraghi's relations with me. Whenever I was not travelling, he would spend time with me almost on a daily basis. Soon I became his confidant. He shared with me information and ideas well beyond my official domain.

The 1970s background of the ILO

Unknown to me, certain developments and events took place at the ILO shortly before my appointment and within the first year of my service that directly or indirectly had a considerable effect on my career.

In July 1970, the newly elected Director-General, Wilfred Jenks, appointed a Soviet citizen, Pavel Astapenko, as Assistant Director-General. As a consequence, the American Congress took a decision to reduce the US contribution to the ILO by 50 per cent. Since the USA provided nearly 25 per cent of the ILO budget and was thus the main contributor, this decision had major negative effects on the Organization's operations and activities. It was only years later that the USA paid the remaining part of its dues.

Wilfred Jenks, who was British, died in October 1973 and was succeeded by Francis Blanchard, a French citizen, who had joined the

Organization in 1951. He became Assistant Director-General in 1956, Deputy Director-General in 1968 and finally Director-General, serving three terms from 1974–89.

Shortly after Blanchard's election, a sequence of events, particularly with regard to Palestine and the occupied Arab territories, further compounded and compromised US–ILO relations. In June 1974, the International Labour Conference (ILC) adopted a resolution concerning the Policy of Discrimination, Racism and Violation of Trade Union Rights practised by the Israeli Authorities in Palestine and the other Occupied Arab Territories.

This was followed by a decision at the same conference to allow the Palestine Liberation Organization (PLO) to participate as an observer at all conferences, meetings and ILO activities. In an official communication on 6 November 1977, the American Secretary of State, Henry Kissinger, gave two years' notice of his country's intention to withdraw from the ILO in accordance with standing procedures.

While Blanchard embarked on an extensive campaign in Europe and elsewhere to dissuade the USA from withdrawing, another resolution was passed by the ILC concerning implications of the Israeli settlements in Palestine and other Occupied Arab Territories.

The menacing consequences of the US withdrawal had an extremely sobering effect on the ILC's and ILO's policies and activities in general. So much so that the 1974 resolution on the Policy of Discrimination, Racism and Violation of Trade Union Rights was annulled by a subsequent session of the ILC.

In recognition of the tangible change in the ILO's policy and direction, the USA – which had joined the ILO in 1934 – announced its return as an active member and honoured its pending dues.

Despite these positive developments, Blanchard was very conscious of the sensitivity the Palestinian issue would continue to pose. He believed that he could deal better with the political issues of the Middle East if its member states were in a separate region. He also had plans to induce the Gulf countries to become members, while acknowledging the almost total absence of trade union rights and freedoms in these states. The concept vis-à-vis the Gulf States was to take them on board and work together to enable them to conform to the ILO standards.

Seizing the opportunity of anticipated partial amendments to the ILO Constitution that primarily concerned the regional structures and allocation of Governing Body seats, Blanchard proposed to create a separate region for the West Asian countries to be headed by an Assistant Director-General. Prior to the proposal made by Blanchard, Arab countries in West Asia were part of the 'Europe and Middle East' region, while Arab States in Africa were members of the African region. The Arab States were given the option either to form a united group or to keep the status quo for the African Arab countries.

Following extensive deliberations, the Arab Labour Ministers concluded that it would be in their interest to be represented in two regions. Accordingly, the newly established region embodied only the West Asian Arab countries and became part of the Asia and Pacific region. As a consequence, the ILO Office in Beirut became the Regional Office for Arab States.

It is worth mentioning that representatives of Arab governments, employers and workers remain in a state of denial with regard to this development. To this day, they continue to request unification of the Arab countries in one regional group at almost every meeting they convene on the occasion of the ILC or the Governing Body. They have never, however, placed this item on the agenda of the Arab Labour Conference in order to present it officially to the ILO.

In due course, during my term in office as Assistant Director-General, I resolved sensitivities over this issue by arranging with the Assistant Directors-General for Africa to allocate funds from both our regular budgets for activities that were earmarked for the tripartite constituents for all Arab countries.

An interesting occurrence that remains vivid in my mind, during the discussion of the changes in the membership of the regions, relates to Israel, which had been a member of the Europe and Middle East region. According to the new set up, it was proposed that Israel would become member of the Europe region. While this subject was being discussed at the Governing Body, a senior and well-informed member of the DG's Cabinet seated by my side passed to me a handwritten 'confidential' note stating that the European countries were strongly resisting the inclusion of Israel in their region. Blanchard's position was quite categorical that no other option was feasible. Hence, the proposal was adopted.

Participation in an ILO delegation to Saudi Arabia

All along I had envisaged my future in the ILO within the area and scope of press and information. I never imagined that I would have the opportunity to be associated with the political aspects of the Organization. I was immersed in my work. My one and only aim and objective was to obtain a contract without a time limit to ensure long-term security for my family and myself.

The only change that concerned me was the departure of JW from the ILO early in 1974. He was replaced by Kyril Tidmarsh, a Briton, who had previously occupied the post of Head of the Office of the Director-General until Jenks passed away.

Hence, I was totally oblivious of the most remote possibility that the aforementioned changes and events could have an effect on my future or that I would be part of the jigsaw or newly created mosaic for the Arab States. With the unfolding of events, fate and destiny were factors that made what seemed impossible happen by total surprise.

In 1975, the Director of the ILO Beirut Office, Dr Saleh Burgan, whose secretary was my sister, was appointed Assistant Director-General (ADG) for the Arab States. Several months later Blanchard decided to visit Saudi Arabia. Much importance was given to the visit being the first ever to be undertaken by an ILO Director-General to the Kingdom. The Minister of Labour at the time, Sheikh Ibrahim Al-Ankari, was a senior member of the Saudi cabinet and enjoyed influence among the Gulf Ministers of Labour.

How well I remember the morning when Al-Maraghi phoned to tell me he wished to see me urgently. The immediate thought that came to my mind was that a decision was taken to suppress my post, as part of the cuts in staff as a consequence to the reduction of the US contribution. I was relieved to note a smile on his face as he asked me to be seated. He lost no time in informing me that he had received a memorandum from the Office of the Director-General informing him that I had been appointed as a member of the ILO delegation to accompany Blanchard on his visit to Saudi Arabia.

Al-Maraghi underlined over and over how privileged I was to have been chosen. Our meeting lasted more than half an hour, during which he spoke at length about his long-standing relations with Blanchard and the good contacts he enjoyed with the hierarchy at ILO headquarters. Within minutes of my return to my office, almost every staff member came to congratulate me for the honour of the foreseen mission with the DG.

While I was pleased and flattered by the news, it was the reaction of Al-Maraghi and the staff that made me fully appreciate the importance of the event. However, I did not realize at that time the profound change that that decision would have on my career and life. In fact, that day marked a new direction in my professional career and brought about the most unexpected and unforeseen evolution in my status as an official of the ILO.

I arranged to be in Riyadh two days before the arrival of Blanchard, to undertake the necessary preparatory work for the visit. Unlike the case in most of the Arab countries, my contacts with the Saudi media were limited. The television and radio stations were run by the government, as was the case of most of the newspapers.

By chance, I came across one of the most senior officials at the Ministry of Information, an Egyptian national, who had worked for the Associated Press in Cairo and whose director at the time was an Al-Dajani. He sang praises of that relationship and was appreciative of the assistance and support he received from my relative. Ironically, I did not personally know the individual concerned nor could I trace our family links! As a result of that encounter, I had direct access to the key figures in the media – television, radio and press.

My first meeting at the Ministry of Labour was with one of the under-secretaries, Sheikh Mohamed Al-Fayez. He was the Ministry's appointed official to accompany Blanchard and the ILO delegation. His warm and friendly reception was a prelude to what became a lasting and close work relationship between us over two decades, covering the years when he later served as the Minister of Labour. Sheikh Al-Fayez briefed me on the programme of the two-day visit, underlining the importance it was being accorded by the Kingdom's leadership. He was pleased with the arrangements I had made for the coverage of the event by the local media.

The scene of Blanchard's arrival remains vivid in my mind. A high-level delegation of no less than 20 officials, headed by the Labour Minister

Sheikh Ibrahim Al-Ankari, were on the tarmac as Blanchard emerged from the aircraft. As he descended the stairs, followed by Dr Burgan and François Tremeaud from his cabinet, the wave of Saudi officials in their national attire advanced to greet them.

I had never met either Blanchard or Tremeaud. Dr Burgan was the only person with whom I once had a brief encounter during a visit I had made to Beirut nearly two years prior. I hardly had time to shake hands with Blanchard, who was oblivious of my identity, before everyone hurried to find a seat in one of the long line of limousines making ready to leave for the hotel. The Minister accompanied Blanchard. Sheikh Al-Fayez departed with Dr Burgan and Tremeaud and I found myself with an under-secretary and two other officials from the Ministry.

Arriving at the hotel, there was a brief meeting in the lobby during which time the Minister presented Blanchard with the official programme for the visit. I was summoned by Dr Burgan to join the group and it was at that time that I was officially introduced to the Director-General as well as to Tremeaud. Following the departure of all the government officials, we briefly went over the programme. I had the opportunity to brief everyone present on the arrangements I had made for the media coverage of the visit. Blanchard demonstrated particular interest in what I said. He was delighted to learn I had arranged for him to have an interview with the television as well as the leading English-language and Arabic daily newspapers. That evening, a lavish dinner in honour of Blanchard was hosted by Minister Al-Ankari and was attended by almost all cabinet ministers and dignitaries, including prominent figures of the private sector.

The programme of the visit was extensive, covering key areas and activities that fall within the competence of the ILO. We visited several vocational training centres, technical schools and centres for the disabled. We also visited the Ministry of Labour and Social Affairs. Blanchard showed particular interest in the structure of the Ministry. During the visits, he constantly remarked on how the ILO could provide technical assistance to improve conditions, including structural and capacity building.

The most interesting visit was one to Aramco Oil Company. We were flown by private jet to witness the operation of that gigantic city.

Sheikh Al-Fayez emphasized to Blanchard that such a visit required the approval of the highest officials in the Kingdom and was granted only to selected VIPs. The flight gave me the opportunity to acquaint myself better with Blanchard and Tremeaud. Sheikh Al-Fayez would occasionally point out landmarks of interest on the route, otherwise he would exchange pleasantries with Dr Burgan as their relationship became less formal. Several meetings were held between Blanchard and Sheikh Al-Ankari. To my surprise, I was asked to be present with the other members of the delegation. I was able to experience the tremendous ability of Blanchard to evaluate the situation, and to present in a most subtle and palatable manner the numerous and important advantages the Kingdom received by joining the ILO. Prior to our departure, Al-Ankari hosted a lunch for Blanchard during which the mood and environment that prevailed was indicative of the friendly and positive outcome of the visit.

That evening, Blanchard and the three of us had an early dinner at the hotel. By that time, he was calling me by my first name. He expressed interest in my background and in all that I was doing in the Cairo Office. I should also mention that from the outset of the visit, Tremeaud and I formed a good relationship, which was consolidated during the mission. Thanks to Dr Burgan, I became an integral part of that high-level delegation. His constant words of praise and support made me feel at ease and comfortable rubbing shoulders with the ILO leadership.

The morning of Blanchard's departure was even more ceremonial than his arrival. Besides Al-Ankari and senior officials of his Ministry, a large number of other dignitaries were present. Blanchard was given a memorable farewell. While he and his entourage headed to Geneva, I took the flight back to Cairo.

Reminiscing on my thoughts during my return trip, I remember well the strange feeling I entertained at the airport immediately after the departure of the delegation from Geneva. Within minutes, the hustle and bustle vanished from the VIP departure lounge, leaving me with a sentiment of abandonment. During the three days, I had grown accustomed to the rhythm and style of the mission with all its ceremonial pomp. While being fully aware of the reality of the occurrence, somehow the event left me with a feeling of fantasy and make-believe.

I envisaged what was awaiting me at the Cairo Office and the barrage of questions that I would face from Al-Maraghi and my colleagues. By the time I arrived at Cairo airport, I somehow had the ability to turn a new page – that of back to reality. While cherishing every moment of my Saudi mission, I put it behind me and was full of enthusiasm to perform my work as the regional press officer. However, I do not exaggerate when I say it took more than a full week before the 'story' of my mission gradually phased out at the Cairo Office.

Nearly two months elapsed before I received a personal note from Tremeaud thanking me for the 'excellent' job I had done and requesting me to keep in touch. That gesture brought considerable professional satisfaction to me, coupled with a sentiment that I had not been altogether forgotten.

Geneva beckons

During the following year, the Regional Office for Arab States was fully operational under the leadership of Dr Burgan. He was being assisted by a programme officer, Rafiq Teylouni, a Syrian who had been handling the affairs of the West Asian countries in the Europe and Middle East Regional Office that has been dismantled.

On my part, I continued to travel extensively and would participate in the International Labour Conferences and some meetings of the ILO Governing Body. This gave me the opportunity of meeting with my direct Chief, Kyril Tidmarsh, as well as Dr Burgan, Tremeaud and very occasionally Blanchard.

I was also a regular member of the ILO delegation, headed by Dr Burgan, that attended the annual meetings of the Arab Labour Conference. In time, and as a result of these encounters, my relations with Dr Burgan grew stronger. He maintained his attitude of including me in all his high-level meetings and discussions, which provided me with a wealth of experience vis-à-vis relations between the ILO and the Arab countries.

Unknown to me, very discreet discussions were in progress between Blanchard, Dr Burgan and Tidmarsh to have me transferred to Geneva. Their idea was that I would continue with my work as Regional

Information Officer on a 50 per cent basis with the Press Department and would also serve as assistant to Dr Burgan on a part-time basis. The proposal had the full backing and support of Tidmarsh, who stated in my annual report that I 'possessed political acumen', which the ILO should fully utilize.

One morning, Al-Maraghi's secretary phoned me to say he wished to see me urgently. I sensed something was wrong as he usually phoned me directly. Arriving at his office, I was confronted by a frowning person who eyed me with much hostility. His shaking hand was holding a paper, which he literally flung towards me, demanding that I provide an explanation for its contents.

It was a memorandum from the Chief of the Cabinet of the Director-General, Bernard Fortin, informing Al-Maraghi that Blanchard had decided to transfer me to Geneva, with the credits for my post, and that I should report to ILO headquarters within one month. Upon reading the memorandum, I was quite flabbergasted. I asked if I could sit down. I was in a state of shock, which was confounded by Al-Maraghi's state of extreme anger. I was categorical that I knew nothing about this decision. Al-Maraghi's attitude and reaction were cynical. He told me he would oppose the decision and that he was extremely disappointed with the event, clearly insinuating his disbelief in what I said.

The week that followed was an extremely tense and sad period of my service at the Cairo Office. Al-Maraghi's intervention apparently angered Blanchard and resulted in a rather harsh rebuke from the Chief of Cabinet, Bernard Fortin, who addressed the transfer orders directly to me. In the days that followed, I spared no effort to convince Al-Maraghi that I was equally surprised by the decision and was unaware of it. Much to my delight and satisfaction, his attitude towards me assumed normality when he became convinced that I was not party to the 'plot'.

I had maintained more than good relations with Al-Maraghi throughout the years I served in the Cairo Office. He was a man of considerable experience from which I profited professionally. Most importantly, I certainly was the only official in whom he confided and I was determined to retain our friendship and mutual respect.

It was during our last meeting in his office, prior to my departure, that he told me that the private and personal enquiries he made confirmed the validity of my version about the transfer. To my great surprise, he apologized to me for his attitude. He embraced me and wished me success in my new job. My relief was immense. I was now able to leave Egypt with nothing but good memories for Al-Maraghi and all the colleagues I served with in Cairo.

My move to Geneva had one aspect that tormented me, that of leaving my aunt Husnieh, who had become an integral part of my daily life and that of my family. She was a source of strength and inspiration to me. Her love and affection were the healing factors that enabled me to overcome the sudden and tragic departure of my father. She and I would play cards until the early hours of the morning. She would tell me stories about my father's youth, how he would confide in her on all matters and the special bond between them.

Departing from her was indeed such sweet sorrow. Sad as I was, I was certain she would visit us regularly. Equally important, she was so overwhelmed with happiness for my new position that she rejoiced at my departure.

Arriving in Geneva with my wife and two daughters marked a new era in my life at all levels. Professionally, I felt more stable and secure. My transfer was not only an acknowledgement of my performance but, more importantly, it provided me with the opportunity to progress in my career development.

At the family level, we were able to enjoy the peaceful and beautiful environment of an international city. Aida and Karima were overwhelmed by their new academic set up. At the outset, I was slightly concerned about the manner in which I was going to handle my new assignment – to strike a balance between two responsibilities and to satisfy my two superiors. Within weeks of my starting work in Geneva, these concerns were dispelled. Both Dr Burgan and Tidmarsh gave me carte blanche to execute my duties. They entertained no sensitivities between them, granting me the decision to prioritize my work as required.

Burgan, who was a medical doctor by profession and had held several cabinet posts in Jordan, was known for his humility. A Christian, married to a lady of Palestinian origin, he mastered knowledge of the Qur'an, whose verses he regularly recited and used to punctuate his statements and speeches.

The ILO Regional Office for Arab States

It is worth noting that the appointment of Dr Burgan envisaged that he would be posted in Beirut from where he would run the entire operation of the Arab States in West Asia. However, the precarious security situation in Lebanon at the time prompted Blanchard to retain him in Geneva at the outset.

In essence, Burgan's main responsibility focused on the political aspects of the ILO's work in the West Asian countries. The Beirut Office, which was undertaking the technical cooperation activities, was also directly under his authority. Burgan entrusted Teylouni with handling that part of the operation. He would intervene only when major decisions were required.

From the outset, Burgan made it clear that I would be his main assistant and adviser on political matters. What I never expected was my immediate and direct involvement in the political and policy issues at the level of the directorate. Burgan became my mentor. To him I owe eternal gratitude for providing me with the opportunity and chance to progress in my career at the ILO.

I should mention at this stage that the issue of Palestine, with varying degrees of intensity, was omnipresent in almost all ILO activities throughout my career. My Palestinian origin forced me to walk on a tight rope whenever dealing with Palestinian affairs. I drew strength and motivation from this challenge. With time, I learned the art of handling this sensitive and thorny subject with firmness and conviction. I was categorical about the need to recognize the full rights of the Palestinians, through the process of upholding ILO standards. Despite the extremely stormy and turbulent periods which the Office and I in particular encountered over this issue, throughout my career, ironically it was instrumental in revealing and highlighting my ability to overcome and resolve complex conflicts among the adversaries.

Following my retirement from the ILO, in 1997, I was appointed by Royal Decree Honorary Counsellor for ILO Affairs at the Jordan Permanent Mission in Geneva. Hence, continuity remains in my association with this subject to this day. As to the circumstances of this appointment, I will revert to it in due course at the appropriate juncture.

Crown Prince Hassan of Jordan

A significant event that needs to be chronicled was the visit of Blanchard to Jordan in February 1977. I was a member of the delegation accompanying the Director-General. One morning, we had a meeting with Crown Prince Hassan, who briefed us on the situation in Palestine. I vividly recall him pointing to the maps and charts and telling Blanchard that the main threat to future peace and stability was the policy of Israel to construct settlements in Palestinian territory. While stating that only a handful had been established by that time, 'it was a cancer that would spread with devastating effect.' These were his exact words. Few people, including Blanchard, acknowledged the vision and far-sightedness of Prince Hassan at the time.

That evening, while the Director-General was dining with Prince Hassan, news of the tragic death of Queen Alia in a helicopter crash was announced. The following day, Blanchard and the delegation attended the funeral in the palace grounds before returning to Geneva. I recall that President Assad of Syria was present at the ceremony.

In June of the same year, Prince Hassan was guest of honour at the 63rd Session of the International Labour Conference. His address on that occasion was memorable. Speaking on the critical issue of the brain drain, which was inflicting serious socio-economic damage on many countries including Jordan, Prince Hassan proposed the establishment of an international compensation fund to be financed by labour importing countries in favour of states that supplied the manpower.

The idea was stillborn. It was rejected outright by the Gulf States and disappeared from the annals of the ILO.

Visits to and reports on the Occupied Territories

The ILO is the only UN organization which Israel allows to undertake annual missions to examine the conditions of Palestinian workers and employers under occupation, in accordance with a resolution that was adopted by the International Labour Conference in 1978.

The exercise entails sending two missions. One goes to the Arab frontline countries, namely Jordan, Syria and Egypt, to gather information on the situation. This mission also used to meet with the representatives of the Palestine Liberation Organization, the Arab League and the Arab Labour Organization. The other visits Israel where it presently meets with representatives of the Palestinian authority as well as the workers and employers. It also meets with Israeli officials. The information obtained by both missions is then compiled in a special report, which the Director-General presents annually to the ILC on the conditions of workers in the Occupied Territories.

From 1982 until my retirement in 1997, I was member of the two-person team that undertook the mission to the frontline Arab countries. The second member of the team was always the Chief of the Equality and Rights Branch at the ILO.

A memorable yet tragic incident took place during one of my missions to Syria with Claude Rossillion, a Frenchman, who headed the aforementioned Branch. The two of us were in an official car on our way to meet the Minister of Labour in his office in Damascus.

I well recall we were in the middle of a main avenue when a huge ball of fire, three stories high, engulfed the entire road and buildings some 100 metres ahead. Seconds later, we heard a deafening explosion and saw the fire swallowing cars and humans, who were ahead of us. Our car was literally catapulted one metre above ground. Our driver was able to make a U-turn and speed away from the scene.

Claude became hysterical. He was shaking, repeatedly saying he wanted to return to Geneva. We had witnessed one of the deadliest terrorist attacks by the Muslim Brotherhood group against the regime of Hafez Al-Assad. Nearly 100 people were killed and several hundred injured. At Claude's insistence, we went back to the hotel. He was visibly shocked. He phoned his wife, recounting the event and informing her that he was returning immediately. There were no flights from Damascus to Europe that day. Considering his state, I arranged transport for him to Beirut by car and requested the ILO Office there to arrange for his onward journey to Geneva.

I have wondered at the vast difference in the reaction of Claude and myself to the incident. My experiences as a child in Palestine encountering death, bloodshed and violence as well as in Lebanon and elsewhere in the Middle East rendered me relatively immune to such emotional reactions. In fact, I noted that I had developed a trait of toughness in the face of such situations.

Another historic event relating to the report of the Director-General took place in 1982, when a prominent Swiss official of the ILO with the rank of Assistant Director-General, Mrs Antoinette Béguin, headed the team charged with the preparation of the report. Upon release of the report, I was told by a senior member of the cabinet that the Israeli government officially transmitted its discontent over its 'tone and contents'. Matters were further compounded by a footnote that was inserted in the final text and which had not been included in the advance copy that was circulated to the concerned parties.

The footnote referred to serious occurrences that took place on the West Bank and East Jerusalem subsequent to the completion of the report. The footnote said:

> Following, in particular, the removal from office of elected mayors on the West Bank, demonstrations and strikes spread to the main towns and localities. The occupation authorities took various repressive or restrictive measures affecting, directly or indirectly, the Arab workers and the functioning of their economy, trade union and municipal institutions.

The footnote concluded by stating that the Director-General personally approached the government of Israel, 'expressing in particular the wish that the abovementioned measures be lifted and requesting the Government to furnish all relevant information as soon as possible'.

One morning, Dr Burgan and I were informed that Blanchard wished to meet with us urgently. I noted that he was visibly disturbed as he greeted us. He confirmed that the government of Israel had expressed its 'rejection of the report'. He revealed that he had met the evening before with the Israeli Ambassador at the hospital where he was waiting to be operated on. The Ambassador wanted the assurance of Blanchard that Mrs Béguin would never again be associated with the reports on the Occupied Territories. Blanchard told us he gave his assurance to that effect. Henceforth, Mrs Béguin was totally dissociated from all matters pertaining to the Occupied Territories. This incidence in no way reflects upon the calibre and competence of Mrs Béguin, an excellent ILO official by all accounts. Rather it reflects upon the strongly interventionist approach of Israel regarding the ILO's work relating to Palestine and the Occupied Territories.

The issue of Palestine became critical for the ILO, particularly vis-à-vis its relations with the United States. Blanchard was determined to defuse the tension that had engulfed the ILO's environment with regard to this issue.

In January 1979, Blanchard undertook a 14-day mission to Syria, Jordan, Iraq, Kuwait and Qatar. He was accompanied by Dr Burgan, a member of his cabinet and myself. The prime objective of the mission was to inform the leadership of these countries about the situation pertaining to America's resumption of its active membership at the ILO. He urged cooperation and avoiding escalation of the confrontation over the issue of Palestine.

Blanchard assured that the ILO would continue to monitor the situation in the Occupied Territories, that he would submit annual reports to the Conference each year and that technical assistance would be provided to the Palestinians. During these visits, Blanchard met with almost all heads of states of the countries in question, as well as the prime ministers, senior dignitaries and representatives of the employers and workers. There was consensus among the visited countries to protect and preserve the interest of the ILO while underlining the need to ensure that this was not done at the expense of the Palestinian cause. However, the aforementioned positions were expressed in varying levels of rigidity and flexibility.

It was unprecedented for any Director-General to undertake such a long mission to any region. Of all the missions that I undertook with Blanchard and other Directors-General, this one revealed to me the realities of what is said behind closed doors as opposed to in public.

I was impressed by the ability of Blanchard to manoeuvre his way through delicate and sensitive discussions, almost always emerging as the friend and ally. That mission was, in fact, a milestone in the relations between Blanchard and the Arab countries.

Diminishing importance of the Palestinian issue

It is important to note the major diminishing importance which the Palestinian issue has witnessed at the ILO over recent years, as a direct result of fragmentation of Arab unity and the socio-political turmoil that has dawned over the region during the last two decades.

As indicated earlier, Palestine was a central issue at the ILO from the mid-1970s to the late 1980s. It featured prominently in discussions of the Governing Body and was the cause of paralysing the work of the 'Resolutions Committee', thereby disabling the Conference from achieving its objectives. Discussions on the Director-General's report on the Occupied Arab Territories at the ILC were politically charged, leading to extreme tension among delegations and serious concern by the Office regarding the negative reaction from major donor countries.

With time, the Resolutions Committee was suppressed and a Special Sitting was established at each ILC to discuss the DG's report on the Occupied Territories, whereby delegations were forbidden from making any reference to Palestine in the plenary of the ILC.

After a few years, the Arab Group realized the futility of the Special Sitting. In fact, it was tantamount to a reunion of the Arab tripartite constituents and their supporters, who delivered fiery speeches, the echoes and effect of which remained within the limits of the assembly hall. Consequently, the Special Sitting was terminated and the Director-General's report on the Occupied Territories resumed being discussed at the plenary.

In contrast to the past, statements on this subject are now brief and moderate. In fact, many Arab delegations make no more than a fleeting mention of Palestine in their interventions.

This aspect of ILO work has continued without interruption, even after the establishment of the Palestinian Authority. In fact, during the mandate of the current Director-General, Guy Ryder, the report has become more forceful and critical about the continuing deteriorating conditions of workers and employers in Palestine. It highlights the negative effects of the establishment of settlements and openly speaks of the need to end occupation and to seek a negotiated settlement on the basis of a two-state solution.

Ironically, though the reports of the Director-General on the Occupied Territories became more vocal and critical of Israel and its policy of occupation, the government now has a fairly passive attitude towards the exercise. It has come to realize that the report vents the anger and frustration of the Arabs and their supporters during the few days of its discussion at the ILC. Admittedly, its contents chronicle serious acts and practices on the part of Israel, yet these would in reality be mere ink on paper with regard to tangible consequences.

Appointment as Director of the ILO Office in Beirut

Following the assignment of Dr Burgan to Geneva, the post of Director of the ILO Office in Beirut remained vacant for nearly two years. International officials serving at the office were alternately named as acting directors. The office environment was not wholesome and the security situation in Lebanon was deteriorating. Dr Burgan mentioned on several occasions that Blanchard 'expressed frustration' over the lack of management and control at that office, indicating the need to make radical changes to its operation. To my knowledge, Dr Burgan was actively prospecting for a new Director. I was least concerned about this matter, being totally active and content with my assignment.

One morning, Dr Burgan's secretary informed me that he wished to see me urgently. He was particularly cold in his reception when I entered his office. He asked if there was something important of which I should have informed him. Puzzled, I said no. He repeated the question twice over while receiving the same response from me.

To my utter shock and amazement, he told me that Blanchard had decided to appoint me as Director of the ILO Beirut Office. He had clearly found it 'strange' that I was totally unaware of my nomination. He recounted that during the meeting of the Senior Management Committee (SMC), held that morning, one of the agenda items was the Beirut Office. Blanchard apparently informed the committee members that he had decided to appoint me as Director of that office with immediate effect. He had not consulted Burgan who, understandably, as my superior and mentor wished to ensure I was not party or accomplice to this decision.

The announcement had considerable reverberations, both at ILO headquarters and the Beirut Office. Several Arab staff members in Geneva who aspired for the post were disappointed. In fact, one of them told Deputy Director-General Bertil Bolin, who was responsible for field operations, that the Lebanese government would not accept my

24. The author with Aziz Al-Maraghi, Director of the ILO
Office in Cairo.

25. Director-General of the ILO Francis Blanchard, Dr Saleh Burgan and the author
at a vocational training centre in Riyadh during an official visit to Saudi Arabia.

26. Blanchard in a private jet heading to ARAMCO Oil Company with Under-Secretary of Labour Sheikh Mohamed Al-Fayez, Saleh Burgan and the author.

27. Francis Blanchard and the author meeting with Iraqi Minister of Labour Bakar Rasoul in Baghdad, 1978. Rasoul was instrumental in a US$1 million contribution from Iraq to the ILO to introduce Arabic as an official language.

28. The author with the Secretary-General of the International Confederation of Arab Trade Unions (ICATU), Hassan Jamam. A working relationship that sparked new dynamics between ICATU and the Gulf States.

29. Blanchard with Syrian Minister of Labour Yusif Jedani during his tour of West Asian countries in 1979, with the author in the centre. Syria was a key player within the Arab group at the ILO.

30. Meeting between Blanchard, the author and HRH Prince Hassan in Amman in 1977. 'Settlements will become a major problem.'

31. Photograph given to the author by Yvette Verchère, special assistant to Blanchard, showing the Director-General with the author at the Asian Regional Conference in Jakarta in 1993. 'You two have so much in common.'

32. Meeting with Secretary-General of the United Nations Javier Pérez de Cuéllar in Tunis, 1980.

33. The author being received by President Amine Gemayel of Lebanon at the Ba'abda Presidential Palace.

34. The author during one of his regular meetings with Chairman Yasser Arafat to discuss the ILO technical assistance programme for the Palestinians.

35. The author greeting HRH Prince Talal Bin Abdel Aziz Al-Saud at the ILO headquarters in Geneva for high-level discussions on cooperation between the ILO and AGFUND.

36. Audience with President Suharto of Indonesia in 1993.

To Mr. Shukri Dajani,
with appreciation of all
your positive
efforts and the
human that
facilitates
them.
Basma
March 1996.

37. An autographed photo presented to the author by HRH Princess Basma of Jordan in acknowledgement of the assistance the ILO provided to her non-governmental organization.

38. The author with Director-General Hansenne, being received by Deputy Prime Minister of Oman Fahd bin Mahmoud Al-Said during their official visit to the Sultanate in 1995.

39. The author in the company of HM King Hussein, enjoying a get-together on the occasion of an Old Victorians reunion.

nomination because of my Palestinian origin. In Beirut, an atmosphere of frustration and rejection of my nomination was openly voiced by some senior members of the staff, on the grounds that they were more qualified and experienced. It is with this background and the consequential implications and challenges that I decided to undertake my new responsibilities.

I had a meeting with Blanchard almost two weeks following the official announcement. By that stage, Dr Burgan had realized that I had been as unaware of my appointment as he had been, and our good relations were re-established. Blanchard was evidently aware of the 'shockwaves' his decision had created. He expressed confidence in my ability to 'impose authority and good functioning' of the office and assured me of full support from headquarters. One thing that was evident and clear is that Blanchard was ready to take unilateral decisions regardless of the SMC and the direct chiefs concerned, which in my case was Dr Burgan.

At the time, Lebanon was passing through an extremely difficult and complicated political and security situation. The Palestine Liberation Organization (PLO) had established its base in Lebanon following its ousting from Jordan. Military factions of the PLO had control of certain areas of the country, a situation that created tension and friction with the Lebanese Army and political parties and militias opposing Palestinian presence.

Facing the challenge

Within a month of the announcement of my appointment as Director of the ILO Office in Beirut, in March 1979, I was heading to Lebanon anticipating possible problems on many fronts. One consolation was that Marwan Nasser, a prominent Lebanese employer member of the ILO Governing Body, had contacted me by telephone a few days before my departure, to express his support and that of the government for my nomination. The timing of that message was crucial. It enabled me from the outset to concentrate my efforts on the affairs of the office and the process of its reform. I had no qualms about the handling of staff or management of the office. I was more concerned about re-establishing a reputable status for the Beirut Office soonest, at the regional level.

During the flight, I thought of my wife and two daughters whom I had left behind in Geneva. They were to follow me once I had settled down in my new job.

As the flight was approaching the airspace of Greece, the pilot announced that he was obliged to land in Athens because of an intense Israeli air raid on Beirut city and the airport. We were obliged to spend the night in Athens. Communications with Lebanon were disrupted. I was not able to contact the ILO representatives nor the government officials who were supposed to meet me upon arrival. This dramatic and unorthodox welcome to my new post prepared me for the difficult task that lay ahead.

The next day, I arrived in Beirut unannounced and unnoticed. I certainly did not wish to occupy officials at the Ministry of Labour with my affairs at such difficult times, nor did I wish to have any of the ILO staff risk going to the airport under the prevailing precarious conditions.

Naturally, I was in constant contact with Dr Burgan who transmitted information about my movements to the concerned officials at ILO headquarters. The Israeli attack caused considerable damage to the airport and to various locations throughout the city. It was the following day that I went to the office. Contrary to my expectations, I had an extremely warm reception by all the staff, professionals and local.

Before noon, I was informed by the Ministry of Labour that the Minister would visit me at the office and would later host me for lunch. The arrival of the Minister together with the Director-General of the Ministry, Hameed Khoury, as well as Marwan Nasser and the Minister's special adviser Ma'arouf Suwaid had a special and lasting effect on all the staff. It was the first time ever that such a high-ranking national delegation had come to the ILO Office. Thus, that day marked a turning point in the status of the office and a new era in the relationship between the ILO and the Lebanese tripartite constituents.

While appreciating and acknowledging these unexpected positive developments, I was fully aware of the mammoth task that confronted me to concretize the capacity of the office to provide the appropriate and adequate technical assistance to the constituents in West Asia. Within weeks, the dynamics of the office witnessed a dramatic change. My intensive meetings with the professional and local staff yielded immediate positive results. An active and friendly environment dawned whereby everyone performed their jobs with interest and enthusiasm. For the professional staff, work programmes were established for countries of the region and deadlines were set for their accomplishment. Prior to my arrival to Beirut, I had an apprehension about abandoning the press aspect of my work, which was a pivotal part of my career at the ILO. To my amazement, I found myself savouring the managerial and political aspects of my new job in preference to that of the media.

The security situation in Lebanon was extremely precarious. The presence of armed factions of the PLO, together with the Lebanese militias and the Syrian presence sparked constant clashes between the adversaries. Bomb explosions and the sounds of gunfire were almost daily occurrences, with various degrees of intensity.

The decision to bring my family to Lebanon was difficult and arduous. Despite the danger involved, I decided to have them join me, knowing that I would be in that post for several years. It was comforting for us all to be together. I should mention that both my sisters lived in Beirut at that time as well as a fair number of relatives. As mentioned earlier, my sister Farihan, who was secretary to Dr Burgan, remained in that function after his departure, serving the various acting directors. My arrival created a problem as I considered it inappropriate to retain her as my secretary. Following intense negotiations with her, she was ready to sacrifice for me by accepting my appointing another staff member as my secretary, while she retained the post of senior secretary.

Ironically, the same scenario was repeated when I was appointed Assistant Director-General, as she had been the secretary of my predecessor. It was easier to resolve that problem at headquarters. She was transferred to the Bureau for Workers' Activities (ACTRAV) as secretary to the Director.

Her replacement was Rita Khavesian, who had served at the Beirut Office. Rita was exemplary in every sense and remained in that post until my retirement.

During my first year in Beirut, I travelled extensively in the region with the objective of consolidating relations with the tripartite constituents. I also developed joint programmes with the Arab Labour Organization, the International Confederation of Arab Trade Unions and the Arab

Chamber of Commerce and Industry. Often, during my missions, I would be accompanied by multi-disciplinary teams of experts from the Beirut Office and headquarters to identify and formulate project proposals.

Within a year, the Beirut Office had regained its credibility and status in the region as well as at ILO headquarters. During my mission to Geneva to attend the International Labour Conference in 1980, Blanchard congratulated me on a 'job well done'. We had a lengthy meeting during which I briefed him on my future plans of action and he provided me with some guidelines on issues of concern to the ILO. Palestine and freedom of association in the Gulf States featured prominently in our discussion. Dr Burgan was equally complimentary about my performance. He was relieved and happy with the positive feedback from the West Asian constituents regarding the Beirut Office.

A major occurrence during my presence in Geneva was the birth of my third daughter Shireen. Though I aspired to have a son, she managed to captivate me from the first sight upon my return to Beirut, leaving me with a sense of guilt for my gender discriminatory attitude.

In retrospect, I realize that I was extremely fortunate to have enjoyed almost total freedom of action as Director of the Beirut Office until 1985 when Dr Burgan retired and Ghaleb Barakat succeeded him as ADG.

My experience in the ILO, particularly at headquarters, made me realize from an early stage the imperative of combating bureaucracy and having the courage to express your views, even if they were not in accord with those of your superiors. The saying 'it is the man that makes the job and not vice-versa' is fully applicable to the United Nations system.

I earnestly believe that the major parts of my achievements at the ILO were the result of my taking unilateral initiatives and decisions and communicating them to my superiors only at times when I deemed it necessary to do so. Needless to say, I was never oblivious to the dangers inherent in this practice and the serious consequences in the event that matters went awry.

In my judgement, a director of a regional office or an ADG is de facto entrusted to protect the interest of the constituents in his/her region as well as that of the ILO. In principle, no conflict of interest exists between the two. Hence, their role is to coordinate, facilitate and consolidate the interaction between the two partners.

Following in-depth analysis of the situation in the Western Asia region, I decided that the ILO's activities should primarily focus on initiating, expanding and consolidating technical assistance to the governments of the region. Another top priority was to defuse the extreme tension between the International Confederation of Arab Trade Unions (ICATU) and the Gulf States and to initiate the process of introducing some form of freedom of association in these countries.

There was a need to consolidate relations and assistance to employers' organizations and then to promote the newly formed ILO project on the development of small- and medium-scale enterprises (SMEs) among them.

Evidently, Palestine was also a key issue. It was the responsibility of the Beirut Office to maintain constant contact with the PLO leadership as well as Palestinian workers and employers and to provide them with technical assistance within the areas of competence of the Organization.

The most challenging and delicate of the above objectives was that concerning the ICATU and the Gulf States. The ICATU had waged an offensive against the Gulf States at the regional and international levels. Complaints for breach of trade union rights and freedoms were regularly lodged at the ILO and other international and regional organizations. The annual meetings of the Arab Labour Conference (ALC) became a forum for confrontation that often went well beyond the limits of diplomacy and protocol. Indeed, the situation had deteriorated to the extent that Sheikh Mohammed Al-Fayez, who at the time was Saudi Minister of Labour, threatened that his country might well withdraw from the ALO. At a meeting held in Baghdad, he reprimanded the ICATU delegates, saying that his country was the main financial contributor to the Organization and all it received in return was criticism and abusive language from the workers.

While the Beirut Office was progressing in assuming an active role among the tripartite constituents in the region, the security situation was in constant deterioration. A dramatic incident that occurred almost two years after my family's arrival portrays best our living conditions at that time.

My wife and I had never taken the risk of going out at night nor of leaving our children in the care of any person, including family members. There was always the likelihood of an outbreak of military clashes and the possibility of being cut off from our neighbourhood. Enjoying a rare period of calm spreading over Beirut for several weeks, we were finally tempted to go out to dinner with my sister Farihan and a few friends to the Summerland Hotel that was a few kilometres from our home. We left our daughters with our neighbours, who were the landlords of the building and had children of the same age as ours.

Arriving at the reception of the hotel, we were told that the main dining room was full. In the typically efficient and practical Lebanese fashion, the manager proposed accommodating us outdoors on the terrace next to the pool and overlooking the sea. As it was a warm spring night, the offer was welcomed by all, particularly as it meant being away from the smokers and loud sound of the orchestra.

We were enjoying the entrées of Lebanese mezze under a star-studded sky, and the sound of the waves breaking on the nearby beach. Suddenly there was a deafening explosion that we felt right over our heads. We were jolted in our seats, as was the table, scattering what was on it in all directions. The hotel premises containing the dining room was on fire with thick smoke billowing, while shattered glass and debris engulfed us and littered the terrace.

A car bomb had been detonated at the entrance of the hotel within proximity of the dining room, causing the death of over 50 persons, with over a hundred injured. We managed to find the exit, having to walk through the debris and the choking dense smoke, amidst the screaming of the injured and a state of panic all around. We mounted the little path to the main road in a state of shock – none of us exchanging a word. Ambulances with their loud sirens engulfed us and their crews rushed towards us, inquiring if we needed assistance. Fortunately, only one person was having a problem in breathing and was given oxygen for a few minutes.

Returning home, our neighbours, who had heard the explosion and were told it was at the hotel where we had gone, reacted as though they were seeing ghosts. Having heard and seen the news coverage of the incident on the local television, they could not believe that we had escaped unscathed from such a huge and deadly explosion.

My wife and I realized how lucky we were. It was not only the fact that we came so close to death but also that our children would have become orphans. Needless to say, we never again went out to dinner during our entire stay in Lebanon.

Evacuation from Lebanon

On 6 June 1982, I was in Geneva attending the ILC when Israel invaded Lebanon from the south. Its offensive by air inflicted major structural damage to Beirut airport, rendering it totally dysfunctional. Ferocious battles took place between the Israeli troops and the military factions of the PLO, who were entrenched in West Beirut. The Syrian army and some units of the Lebanese army as well as a pro-Palestinian Lebanese militia were also engaged in the confrontation with the Israeli troops.

East Beirut was under the control of the Israelis and the Christian Phalangist armed militias. They controlled the port of Jounieh, which was the only outlet from Lebanon. The land route to Syria was under control of the Israeli army and its navy had enforced a total blockade on navigation along the entire Lebanese coast. In addition, the Israeli army and the Phalangist militias had also occupied key and strategic areas in the mountains overlooking Beirut.

Following two weeks of intensive hostilities, which threatened serious consequences on the entire region, the world powers intervened to attempt to resolve the impasse and defuse the explosive situation. A multinational force comprising troops from America, France and Italy was deployed to impose a ceasefire, evacuate foreigners, guarantee a safe passage and departure for Yasser Arafat and his troops, and eventually oversee a withdrawal of Israeli troops from Lebanon.

The United Nations ordered the immediate evacuation of all international officials. The problem was how to conduct the operation, taking into account that the only outlet was the port of Jounieh that was under full control of the Israelis and the Phalangists, who vowed not to allow persons of Palestinian origin to leave the country, irrespective of their current nationality or status.

The United Nations Development Programme (UNDP) Director in Lebanon at that time, Guy Van Doosselaere, was a close friend. We were in hourly contact and he briefed me on developments and plans. Arrangements were made through the French Ambassador in Lebanon, Paul-Marc Henry, to have French marines undertake the evacuation exercise by means of a vessel commandeered by the French Navy. My predicament was that my wife and three daughters as well as my sister (who was being evacuated as a British subject) faced extreme danger of being abducted by the Phalangist militias in their attempts to depart. In fact, the plan was that all UN officials and their dependants would spend a night in East Beirut, for vetting and clearance purposes, prior to being taken by boats to the French vessel the *Azur*.

It did not matter in the least that they were family members of a UN official, nor that my wife was a French national and so were my daughters. The name Al-Dajani was unmistakably Palestinian. That meant they would certainly be prevented from departing and that their fate would be unknown. Guy described to me the situation as one of total 'chaos, brutality and vengeance'. The militias were the power and their weapons ruled throughout the territory. I well remember the cautious assurances given to me by Guy and Ambassador Henry that they would personally escort my family and do all they could to ensure their safe departure.

The White House sent a special envoy, Ambassador Philip Habib, who was assisted by the US Ambassador to Lebanon, Morris Draper, to oversee the situation and assist in its resolution. A political and military committee was established, which comprised the US Ambassadors Habib and Draper and Ambassadors Henry and Olitteri of France and Italy respectively, as well as the military commanders of the three countries.

Following intensive negotiations, the military committee concluded that the French would go into Beirut first and that the Americans would land when Ambassador Habib was satisfied that the evacuation plans were proceeding well and smoothly. The Italians were scheduled to land the day after the Americans. An arbitrary ceiling had been established by Ambassador Habib for the size of the force to be employed: 800 French, 800 Americans and 400 Italians. The plan called for elements of the Multinational Force and the Lebanese Army Forces to be located together at points between the Syrian and PLO forces in West Beirut, and the Israeli and Lebanese Christian Phalangists deployed in East Beirut.

After many aborted attempts to transport the UN and other foreign nationals to East Beirut, as a first phase for the evacuation, the multinational forces were successful in escorting the convoy of buses to the port of Jounieh. They were to spend the night there at a hotel prior to embarking on the French vessel the next morning. Armed Phalangist militias were sequestrating the passports of all evacuees as they descended from the buses. Van Doosselaere and Henry, who vehemently objected to this procedure, were assured that it was for the 'interest and security' of the passengers. Both representatives were fully aware of the dangers and consequences of this act.

Ambassador Henry told my wife not to hand over her passport and that of the children, under the pretext that they were not accessible and that she would deliver them at the hotel. In addition to her stress and fatigue, following weeks of almost sleepless nights amid heavy fighting and bombardment in West Beirut, my wife managed to fend off the numerous attempts to hand over the family passports. I believe a major factor that assisted her in this regard was that she was unmistakably European in looks and hence the militias were not too alarmed. The same applied to my sister.

In the morning, Ambassador Henry was present to oversee the evacuation operation. People were transported by boats to the vessel and Ambassador Henry was personally supervising the arrivals, ensuring that nobody was missing. Just as the vessel was ready to depart, boats carrying Israeli troops and Phalangist militias boarded, requesting to check the passports of all passengers. My wife had no alternative but to hand over her passport. The Phalangist commander ordered that my children be removed from the boat 'because they were Palestinians', while permitting my wife to travel alone. By the account of my wife, Ambassador Henry was quite furious. Invoking the French sovereignty of the vessel, he ordered all the troops to leave the vessel immediately.

To the surprise and amazement of all on board, the Israeli troops and Phalangist militia members immediately disembarked without further discussion! Ambassador Henry will always be remembered by all the evacuees for his extreme diligence and humanity at a time when these qualities were of utmost need and were instrumental in saving lives.

Another notable position taken by Ambassador Henry related to the departure of Yasser Arafat. For several weeks, Ambassadors Habib and Murphy were shuttling daily by helicopter between Beirut and Tel Aviv to negotiate an agreement by which Arafat and his troops would be given safe passage to sail out of Jounieh port on a vessel provided by the multinational forces. The highlight of the evacuation was the departure of PLO leader Yasser Arafat from Beirut. There was some question of whether he was going by helicopter or by ship and, given the volatility of the situation, exactly when and how he was to depart was a closely held secret.

At dawn, *Atlantis*, the ship that was to carry him out, had docked and was ready for Arafat's scheduled appearance at 11am. Arriving on time, when he neared the checkpoint, Arafat got out of his car to accept the flags of several of his PLO units. His entourage was led in by Ambassador Henry and a contingent of French troops with armoured carriers and a truck full of troops. They jumped out on their side of the checkpoint in a manner to protect him and make sure there were no snipers.

At this point, the American commander Lieutenant Colonel Johnston stood in front of the checkpoint, preventing the French troops and the entourage from proceeding further. An extremely heated argument ensued between Johnston and Ambassador Henry in the midst of an armed confrontation between the French and American troops. It was only following a contact which Johnston made by walkie-talkie with Ambassador Murphy, at the request of Henry, that sense and calm prevailed and the evacuation was conducted.

While we celebrated the safe evacuation of our staff and their dependants, we confronted the mammoth task of dealing with their arrival and the numerous administrative, logistical and social problems involved. There was good will and compassion on the part of those who dealt with the evacuation file, yet the bureaucratic system resulted in considerable delays in resolving minor issues thus creating, at times, an unwholesome environment and frustration.

A major concern to me was to ensure that all possible assistance and protection was given to the local staff who were left behind. On this count, the office and UN Security exerted maximum effort and cooperation. Within two months, the Beirut staff and their families had settled in Geneva and the functioning of operations from headquarters was in full steam.

During the ensuing two years, the security situation in Lebanon remained precarious, making it impossible to plan any return of operations to Beirut. Acknowledging the principle that regional offices should operate from the field, Blanchard was constantly reviewing the situation in consultation with Dr Burgan. We were all conscious of the implications and complications that a protracted security problem would have on this case.

Meanwhile Marwan Nasser and Hameed Khoury, who were both members of the Governing Body at the time, were extremely vocal about their rejection of any possible plan to change the location of the regional office. The Lebanese government insisted that operations should continue to be run from Geneva until such time that conditions would permit a return of the office to Lebanon. The French government strongly supported the standpoint of the Lebanese authorities, indicating it would do everything to block any move to the contrary.

An unexpected development with regard to the location of the regional office occurred on 3 February 1984. Blanchard received a detailed proposal from the Tunisian Minister of Social Affairs Mohamed Ennaceur for the establishment of a completely reshaped regional office for the Arab States, to be based in Tunis. The argument was that the Arab League, together with its specialized agencies as well as the regional office of UNESCO and those of a number of other UN agencies, had relocated to Tunis following the Camp David agreement. Mr Ennaceur was a prominent figure within the sphere of the ILO, having headed his country's delegation to several sessions of the ILC and, more importantly, having presided over one of the ILO's most historic events, the World Employment Conference in 1976.

The project was extremely detailed, citing as a prime objective the provision of better services to the entirety of the Arab countries and to closer and more effective coordination with the Arab League. According to the proposal, the existing regional office would be based in Tunis with some technical advisers. Another part of the technical team would be based at the ILO Office in Kuwait, which would become responsible for the Gulf States.

Blanchard sent the proposal to Deputy Director-General Bertil Bolin, requesting him to discuss the plan with Dr Burgan and all concerned officials, and to provide him with the outcome prior to March, when the Governing Body was scheduled to convene. A meeting chaired by Bolin and attended by Deputy Director-General Jain, Dr Burgan, the heads of the Departments of Programme and Personnel and myself was held the following day.

Prior to the meeting, I had fully briefed Dr Burgan on the futility of the proposal. It would lead to the fragmentation of the regional office, rendering it ineffective. Most importantly, the plan would be totally rejected by the Arab countries in both West Asia and Africa. Dr Burgan agreed with my analyses and delegated me to speak on his behalf at the meeting. Jain was the first to speak. He proposed the setting up of a special task force to study all aspects and implications of the proposal. The heads of the Personnel and Programme Departments endorsed Jain's suggestion, adding that several months would be needed to provide a comprehensive response.

My presentation was brief and concise. I argued, point by point, why the plan was totally contrary to the principles of creating an ILO regional office and provided reasons and concrete examples in support of my views. I said the proposal should be rejected. I also suggested that an early response should be given to Mr Ennaceur to avoid possible negative political ramifications in the region. Bolin expressed full support for my position. He said the proposal would create 'havoc' in the Arab region and that he would inform Blanchard accordingly.

I will never forget the moment Dr Burgan and I returned to his office after the meeting to be faced by Marwan Nasser who was raging with anger. The Lebanese government had learned about the Tunisian proposal and was on the warpath. Dr Burgan informed him of the decision that had just been taken, to which he reacted with joy and much appreciation.

Safeguarding local staff

A major preoccupation of mine since our arrival in Geneva was to safeguard the jobs of our secretarial staff, some of whom remained in Beirut, while others fled to other countries. From the outset, I had argued that they should be brought to Geneva to resume their work. Regretfully, the prevailing rules and regulations were invoked by both the Personnel Department and the Staff Union that local staff could not be transferred to headquarters.

After nine months of intensive discussions and negotiations, sense and logic prevailed. The two secretaries who remained in Beirut and the other two who had taken refuge in England with relatives were brought to Geneva to resume work with the regional office. The significance of this development was considerable on the lives of these staff members and their families. Not only were they able to lead normal lives but they were also able to secure the future of their children, who attended academic institutions in Geneva and most of whom later obtained the Swiss nationality.

My success in getting the Beirut secretaries to Geneva was in a way eclipsed by the impossibility of transferring the two drivers and an office boy, who remained in Beirut. I did, however, receive assurances that they would continue to be on the payroll while we were in Geneva. This arrangement was facilitated by the fact that their accumulative salaries due to the prevailing official exchange rate at the time amounted to less than $600 per month.

We were approaching the second year of our evacuation when I received a telephone call at two o'clock in the morning from the office boy, Ali. He was married with five children, the youngest of whom was then three years old, suffering from a deformation of her heart. His voice was so charged with emotion that he made no sense at the outset. After several minutes, I understood that he and the two drivers had been notified by the Personnel Department that the office had decided to terminate their services. They were requested to go by boat to Cyprus where an ILO official would meet them to finalize the 'settlement deal'. The two drivers, who had contracts without limit of time (WLT), would receive a salary of one year each, while Ali, who was on a fixed-term contract, would receive a salary of six months.

The security situation at the time was perilous and there was no possibility of obtaining any form of employment in a country torn by civil war and armed conflicts. Never can I forget the words of Ali: he threatened to kill all the members of his family and commit suicide rather than face humiliation and starvation as a consequence of the Office's decision to terminate his service.

I tried my best to calm his hysterical state, which was a mixture of screaming, crying, pleading and threatening. After nearly 20 minutes, during which I was hardly able to say a few words, Ali calmed down a little and I was able to assure him that I would speak to the Director-General the next morning in order to rectify the situation. The conversation lasted over one hour, by which time he sounded calm and hopeful, his last words being that I was his only hope and saviour.

I was unable to sleep after that call. It sounded like a nightmare, yet its realism was too evident. I was totally bewildered by the news. Could the Personnel Department have taken such a decision and action without the knowledge of Dr Burgan? Would Dr Burgan agree to such action and would he do so without consulting me? All the more that he knew Ali and was fully aware that he was capable of executing his threat.

I was at the office at eight the next morning and left a message with the Cabinet that I wished to see Blanchard urgently. Not to my surprise, Dr Burgan was appalled and angered by the decision that was taken without his knowledge and consent.

Fortunately, Blanchard was in Geneva. I met him upon his arrival at ten o'clock. I informed him of what had happened. He was astounded to learn that the Personnel Department had not consulted Dr Burgan and myself. He asked whether Ali would carry out his threat to which I replied in the affirmative.

Blanchard asked his secretary to get Mr Farr, the Head of the Personnel Department, on the phone. He told Farr to immediately cancel their decisions regarding the termination of the drivers and office boy. He ordered that they remain on the payroll until return of operations of the regional office to Beirut. He further instructed him not to take any action in future pertaining to the Beirut Office without the prior approval of Dr Burgan.

I was able to communicate the good news to Ali before noon that day. Ali and the two drivers returned to work when operations were resumed in Beirut until their retirement. It is so heartening that Ali phones me regularly in Geneva 'simply to hear my voice and express his eternal gratitude'. His daughter underwent heart surgery and is now a healthy university graduate. Ironically, it turned out that the action taken was the outcome of an initiative taken by a senior member of the Personnel Department in order to 'save' some money for the Organization.

Blanchard's third term as Director-General

In 1982, Blanchard decided to present his candidature for a third term as Director-General. To the surprise of many, including Blanchard himself, the head of the ILO International Institute for Labour Studies, Albert

Tevoedjre, a national of the Republic of Benin, also presented his candidature. Blanchard had hoped his re-election would be by simple acclamation, knowing that the majority of the tripartite constituents were in favour of his continuation. Tevoedjre did not represent a formidable opponent but rather an impediment to a foregone conclusion.

I well recall the meeting Blanchard convened with Dr Burgan and myself to discuss the situation. He was in no way concerned by Tevoedjre's action but rather irritated. Directing his question to me, he asked what I could do with regard to obtaining the support of Arab governments. Before I had an opportunity to reply, he presented me with a document saying it may assist in my task. It was a copy of a letter dated 13 July 1982 from the French President Mitterrand to the President of the Republic of Benin.

The letter noted that Blanchard wished to benefit from a new mandate to enable him to complete the reforms in process and that his proposition was favourably received in general. While acknowledging the eminent qualities and wide experience of Tevoedjre, the letter expressed belief that the future of the ILO would be secured if all members had a common stand on this issue.

I informed Blanchard that I was ready to go to Amman to discuss the matter with the highest authorities. The following week, I travelled to Jordan and had a meeting with Prince Zeid bin Shaker, who held the office of Chamberlain to the Royal Palace. The timing of my visit was very opportune. The Governing Body of the Arab Labour Organization was meeting in Cairo within days. Jordan was a titular government member of that body. I suggested to Prince Zeid that Jordan propose tabling an agenda item to express support and endorsement of Blanchard's candidature by the Arab group.

The plan was fully executed. I returned to Geneva with copy of the formal decision taken by the ALO Governing Body as well as copy of a letter from the Minister of Labour to the Foreign Minister informing him of Jordan's move, with a request that Blanchard be notified through the official channels. Tevoedjre withdrew his candidature two days before the election and Blanchard was re-elected.

As mentioned earlier, Blanchard's relations with the Arab countries were consolidated as a result of the visits he undertook to Syria, Jordan, Iraq, Kuwait and Qatar early in 1979. His commitment to present a report on the conditions of workers and employers in Palestine and the other Occupied Territories, as long as the Israeli occupation persisted, meant that he was perceived as a 'friend', who upheld the cause of justice.

Another factor that played a role in sustaining the good relations pertained to the introduction of Arabic as an official language in the ILO. For two decades, the Arab States had been demanding that the Arabic language become an official language in the ILO.

In 1979, Blanchard struck a deal with the Arabs. As the 1980–81 budget had been already approved without including any provision for Arab language services, he undertook to include provision in his programme and budget proposals for 1982–83 for the full range of services required. As a consequence, the 65th session of the ILC held on 26 June 1979 adopted a resolution to that effect. In reality, the resolution stipulated that the Director-General should take measures to provide services in the Arabic language 'as soon as possible and at the latest in 1982'.

Within weeks following the adoption of the resolution, the Iraqi Minister of Labour, Bakar Rasoul, met with Blanchard in Geneva and handed to him a cheque of US$1 million as a donation from his government to enable commencing Arabic services during the current biennium and as a gesture of 'appreciation and good will'.

I should mention that later Rasoul was elected in the late 1980s as Director-General of the Arab Labour Organization and served in this capacity for several terms.

The year 1983 was a special one for me on the personal and family front. On 12 December of that year, my son Zaki, named after my father, was born. This event brought considerable joy to my wife, my family and, I have to admit, above all to me. His birth in Geneva in one sense marked our evacuation from Beirut. At a more important level, it brought home the reality of our diaspora and the imperative of maintaining our family's continuity for future generations.

Major developments occurred at the ILO, which had direct bearing on the Regional Office for Arab States in 1985. Dr Burgan retired and was succeeded by Ghaleb Barakat, a Jordanian diplomat who was previously Permanent Representative of Jordan to the United Nations in Geneva.

Barakat's appointment changed the entire environment of the regional office and its modus operandi. He was alien to the system of tripartism and faced difficulties in adapting, despite his wide experience and good-will. We maintained good personal relations though he, at times, openly expressed resentment that Blanchard and the heads of technical departments contacted me directly and sought my opinion and advice.

A new Director-General – Michel Hansenne

Another key development was the departure of Blanchard and the appointment of Michel Hansenne as Director-General in March 1989.

Hansenne, who had held several ministerial posts in the Belgian government, including that of Minister of Employment and Labour, was the first Director-General of the ILO to assume office after the end of the Cold War.

My relations with both Blanchard and Hansenne were exemplary. The contrast between Blanchard's ILO and that of Hansenne was extreme and reflected in many ways the totally different characters and personalities of the two men.

Blanchard was a suave, charismatic diplomat, whose knowledge of the ILO was profound and extensive. He mastered the art of dealing with the tripartite constituents and maintaining good relations with them. Having served three terms as Director-General, he developed extensive relations worldwide, with heads of governments as well as the leadership of employers and workers.

An extremely straightforward man whose feelings could often be read on his face, Hansenne was the image of a true academician. Diplomacy was not one of his strong traits, yet at times he was willing to accommodate in this regard when necessary. He sought, with all sincerity, to introduce reforms and was conscious of the vacuum left in Blanchard's wake. His academic approach, and at times inflexible position, precipitated tension with the constituents, particularly the employers. He resented favouritism and all forms of manipulation. Hansenne is a man for whom I hold the highest respect and regard. With time, I came to the conclusion that his ideals were obstacles to his success in an environment such as the ILO.

Blanchard is the one who identified me and provided me with the prospects and opportunity to demonstrate my capabilities and excel in my career. I appreciated his intelligence and wit and most of all I admired his skills in diplomacy, from which I benefited considerably.

An event that marked me was the day Blanchard's assistant and confidante, Yvette Verchère, requested that I see her. She greeted me with her habitual friendly smile and asked me to take a seat. Blanchard and I had recently returned from Indonesia where we had attended the ILO regional conference for Asia and the Pacific. She told me Blanchard was very pleased with the outcome of the meeting and that he had praised my performance. Opening a drawer in her desk, she brought out a photo of Blanchard and myself taken in Jakarta. She presented it to me while saying, 'you two have so much in common'.

Hansenne was the person who appointed me as Assistant Director-General in 1990. From the outset, we developed a transparent and solid work relation that, with time, became the envy of all other heads of regional offices.

Hansenne was having serious communication problems with the Assistant Directors-General and vice-versa. Whenever they were in Geneva and met with him, little conversation was exchanged. He expected them to do the talking and provide the information, while they expected to respond to questions.

To defuse this blockage in communication, I proposed to Hansenne that he host a lunch for the Regional Directors outside the ILO premises, whenever they were in Geneva for the Governing Body or other meetings. He agreed to my suggestion and my intimation that he make an effort to be relaxed and informal.

Unknown to Hansenne, I arranged that the cost of the lunch would be shared by us and that he would be our guest. The first luncheon held at La Réserve Hotel was a historic event remembered to this day by the Regional Directors. The environment at the function, which lasted over two hours, was relaxed beyond expectation. I even managed to get Hansenne to drink a glass of white wine instead of the habitual glass of water!

That day marked a turning point in the relations between Hansenne and his team of Regional Directors. It is worth noting that the tradition of these luncheons persisted for the duration of Hansenne's term in office.

My upbringing, culture and nature are that of being loyal and protective to my superiors. In the case of Hansenne, I considered it my duty and responsibility to propose and suggest to him matters that were outside the strict realm of work. This urge was instigated further by his conservative and reserved personality.

In the early days of his term in office, he had instructed that dignitaries visiting him should not be served any drinks or refreshments. I discovered that when one of the West Asian Ministers of Labour paid him a visit. I was astounded and embarrassed when his secretary, Mrs Sarfati, broke the news to me on that occasion. I lost no time in discussing this matter with Hansenne, pointing out that it was an insult in Arab tradition not to be offered tea or coffee by your host. Following a short discussion, he conceded to my request and Arab delegations, as well as other delegations, were then offered drinks when they visited him.

Another issue which I brought up with Hansenne concerned the privacy of my meetings with him. The custom and tradition at the ILO is that the official handling the region in Cabinet would attend meetings held between the Regional Director and the Director-General. I asked Hansenne to agree that we meet one-on-one without the Chief of Cabinet or any other person in attendance, when I considered such an arrangement necessary. The justification was that at times I would communicate a personal or confidential message from a head of state, prime minister, minister of labour or representative of the other two constituents. In such an event, to respect confidentiality, I was duty-bound to report to no other person than the DG, who would naturally have the prerogative himself, to share the information with whomever he wished. He immediately agreed to my request and instructed his secretary to apply that procedure henceforth. This arrangement angered the Chief of his Cabinet, who tried to suppress it, to no avail.

At the beginning of his second term in office, Hansenne held a special meeting with all the Regional Directors requesting each of them to provide him, within a week, with a document containing their perspective on the 'functions, role and responsibilities of an ADG'. That request was ill-timed for me as I was departing the following day for a two-week holiday.

I had no option but to prepare the paper and to send it by facsimile to the Director-General within the deadline he had set. Upon my return, I was informed by my secretary that she had been inundated by requests from the Regional Directors, who wished to have a copy of my 'proposals'. According to the Regional Director for Africa, Eliase Mabere, Hansenne had met with the directors on this subject and announced that my proposals were the 'model' to be applied.

The suggestions contained in my paper were, in essence, what I had been practising and applying in my function. Hansenne's endorsement of my proposals confirmed his policy that Regional Directors should fully assume and practise their responsibilities in accordance with the system of decentralization, without referring to headquarters except in special circumstances.

The invasion of Kuwait and implications for labour

On 2 August 1990, the Iraqi army invaded Kuwait, occupying the entire country within days. On 31 October 1990, the Director-General, Michel Hansenne, received a communication from the Kuwaiti Minister of Labour and Social Affairs, in exile, Sheikh Jaber Abdullah Al-Jaber Al-Sabah. A resolution was attached, pertaining to the invasion, which he wished to place on the agenda of the November Session of the Governing Body (GB) on behalf of the government, employers and workers of Kuwait. On 2 November, the legal adviser, Francis Maupain, sent a memorandum to Hansenne enumerating the procedural difficulties in processing the Kuwaiti complaint.

Among other things, the text and terminology of the complaint did not conform with ILO norms, rendering it unreceivable; and placing it as an urgent item on the agenda involved a deadline of 14 days and the prior approval of the officers of the GB. The Minister could not present the complaint on behalf of the employers and workers, who needed to communicate their position directly to the Organization. I was contacted by telephone by several senior officials from the Kuwaiti Ministry of Labour who had fled to Saudi Arabia as well as the employer member of the GB, Aqeel Al-Jassim, all requesting my assistance to process their complaint. I was also visited by the Ambassador of Kuwait to the UN in Geneva, who earnestly pleaded his country's case, requesting immediate action by the ILO.

I met with the Chief of Cabinet, Bill Simpson, who had considerable experience in his previous job in the area of the application of ILO

Standards. He shared my opinion that we must exert every effort to include the complaint as an agenda item in the forthcoming session of the GB. The intricacies of this task were numerous and too complex to mention in detail. We spent a good part of the day formulating a plan of action and convened several meetings with the Kuwaiti Ambassador, who undertook to immediately respond to all our requests. We then shared our plan with Maupain, who agreed to it but expressed serious doubt that it could be finalized within the procedural deadline.

It was late in the evening when Bill and I met Hansenne to obtain his approval to commence implementation. To our delight, he was pleased with our initiative and gave us the green light to proceed, on condition that we strictly abide by the standing procedures and Maupain's directives in this regard.

I well recall how we worked on the revised text of the resolution until the early hours of the morning. The next day, all documents pertaining to the complaint were finalized in cooperation and collaboration with the Ambassador and action was initiated to obtain the approval of the officers of the GB. The complaint was placed on the agenda of the November session of the GB and a resolution was adopted for immediate ILO action in this regard. The war in Kuwait had a dramatic and tragic impact on hundreds of thousands of foreign workers, who were obliged to flee the country. As the main exit was by land, the exodus of workers headed to Jordan.

The Kingdom established two massive camps to receive the tsunami of refugees and was under tremendous strain to cope with the endless humanitarian, social, medical and logistical problems arising from their influx.

I took the initiative of contacting the Minister of Labour in Amman and arrangements were made for the ILO to assist the Ministry in the process of documenting all the refugees. This process was essential to enable the local authorities to provide the required services. More importantly, it enabled them to coordinate with the respective governments of the refugees to organize their repatriation.

In February 1991, after months of building an international military coalition force, the battle for the liberation of Kuwait commenced. The military action lasted only 100 hours with fleeing Iraqi forces igniting and leaving in their wake massive blazes at Kuwaiti oil wells.

Upon the cessation of the military action, I proposed to Hansenne that he should visit Saudi Arabia and Kuwait. The media reported that the Gulf countries and, in particular, the latter two states had embarked on terminating the contracts of thousands of nationals of countries that purportedly had supported the Iraqi invasion. This action targeted Yemeni, Jordanian and Palestinian workers in particular. I considered it imperative for the ILO, in the person of its Director-General, to waste no time intervening with these countries to halt the punitive and arbitrary action being taken against workers of specific nationalities. Another major objective of the mission was to provide whatever assistance possible for the reconstruction process of the State of Kuwait. Such were the moments and time that ILO action was directly needed.

The military conflict manifested extremely serious and severe political ramifications in the entire region. The labour market in the Gulf States became volatile, causing a threat to the economies of labour-exporting countries in West Asia. It was opportune for the ILO to provide its expertise and assistance to enable the countries of the region to maximize on the benefit of the labour force to both labour importing and exporting states.

I was fully aware of the inherent dangers that faced me as a Jordanian of Palestinian origin in the aftermath of the Kuwaiti affair and the political environment that prevailed in the region. I was also cognizant of the risk I was taking in Saudi Arabia and Kuwait, of them possibly refusing to receive me as a member of the ILO delegation. That delegation would comprise the Director-General, his Chief of Cabinet and myself. I was at the very early stage of my term in office as Assistant Director-General. During the many years of my service as Regional Director, my relations with the Gulf States had become strong and I enjoyed the respect and confidence of the highest authorities. But I needed to discover, in very clear terms, whether the military and diplomatic events in Kuwait would result in a change in attitude towards me as a Jordanian-cum-Palestinian.

Naturally, I raised this matter with Hansenne who, not to my surprise, responded emphatically that he would not undertake any visit without me. Prior to despatching the communications about the Director-General proposed visits to the respective Ministers of Labour, I proposed to Hansenne that we include the United Arab Emirates (UAE) in our programme, noting that the Minister and I had worked closely on the issue of freedom of association in the Gulf States. Another reason was that there were no commercial flights to Kuwait at the time. The UAE was the only country from which private flights could be organized and we hoped arrangements could be made with the Kuwaiti authorities to provide us with such service.

The DG's visit to the Gulf

Within days, Hansenne received responses from all the three Ministers of Labour welcoming the visit. Our first stop was Saudi Arabia, where we were given a warm reception by the Minister of Labour, Sheikh Mohamed Al-Fayez. We were hosted as guests in one of the palaces and full diplomatic honours were accorded to the visit. Sheikh Al-Fayez, with whom I had developed friendly and close relations over the years, went out of his way to make me feel at home.

The following day, we had a meeting with Crown Prince Abdullah, who became King a few years later. The memory of that meeting remains vivid in my mind. Prince Abdullah had an imposing character. His voice was soft but firm. He spoke slowly, making sure that the translator had sufficient time to transmit his remarks in their entirety.

He listened to Hansenne's words with clear interest and had obviously caught the gist of the DG's concern about possible reprisals against workers of specific nationalities as retribution for positions allegedly taken by their countries towards the Kuwaiti invasion. The Crown Prince confirmed there had been cases of summary dismissals of Yemenis, Jordanians and Palestinians and non-renewal of their contracts. He attributed that to the impulsive reaction to the invasion, while pointing out that the Kuwaiti leadership and a vast majority of the population had taken refuge in Saudi Arabia. Prince Abdullah hoped that the experience of Kuwait would serve in consolidating Arab unity once the emotional after-effects of what had happened had faded away. To our surprise, he praised the standard and performance of Jordanian and Palestinian workers, saying that the Kingdom appreciated their contribution to its development process.

That audience crowned the success of Hansenne's visit to Saudi Arabia. He obtained assurances from the highest authorities that the future of tens of thousands of foreign workers was not imperilled by mass deportations. Most interesting were the parting remarks of Prince Abdullah to Hansenne, namely, that his visit would contribute to stabilizing the environment and mood of the labour market.

Our next stop was the United Arab Emirates, where there was no real menace to the foreign workers. We were met at Dubai airport by the Minister of Labour, Saif Al-Jarwan, together with the top brass of his Ministry. Al-Jarwan had kindly arranged for a private aircraft to transport us to Kuwait on the following day. A lengthy meeting was held between Hansenne and Al-Jarwan, during which discussions centred on the prevailing conditions and political environment in the Gulf States in the aftermath of the war in Kuwait.

Al-Jarwan spoke openly against subjecting foreign workers to reprisals, irrespective of their nationality. He admitted that, in some of the Gulf States, a tendency existed to repatriate nationals of countries that did not openly support Kuwait but was reassuring that this trend was transitional and of limited duration.

I will forever remember the remarks which Al-Jarwan made to Hansenne during the dinner he hosted for us that night. He told the Director-General that I was the ideal person to handle the crises that existed among the West Asian countries in all areas that concerned the ILO. Al-Jarwan's remarks caught me by utter surprise.

I spent considerable time in my room that night wondering about the reception I would face next morning upon arrival in Kuwait. I was fully conscious of the highly charged emotions of the Kuwaitis, at all levels, against the Jordanians and Palestinians. Although my relations with the Kuwaiti tripartite constituents were good at all times, I was not certain they would endure the pressure and tension of the events. I entertained some doubts about being confronted by an unfriendly reception, yet this added to my resolve and confidence. Fear was always alien to my character and culture. Throughout my life, I expected to be judged by my actions and deeds. This trait was the major source of my strength and inspiration. Hence, the closer I got to Kuwait, the more comfortable I was and the more I looked forward to the visit.

Before sleeping, I recalled the remarks which Al-Jarwan made to Hansenne about me. Somehow, I felt that they embodied a message of assurance for me. Incredible as it may seem, on our return trip from Kuwait, Al-Jarwan confirmed the validity of my intuition in this regard. He said his words were meant to dismiss any concerns which I may have had about my visit to Kuwait!

As our flight approached Kuwait City, a layer of black smoke covered the sky. The pilot had warned that we would encounter some turbulence, with assurances that it would cause no danger to us. Looking from the windows, we saw endless oil wells blazing with fire, sending thick black smoke spiralling for thousands of feet in the already grey and black sky. The sight left the three of us tongue-tied while exchanging expressions of shock on our faces.

We disembarked from the aircraft to be greeted on the tarmac by a dozen officials headed by the Minister of Labour and Social Affairs, Ahmad Kuleib, a stocky, bearded man, who had been recently appointed. I noted that the reception committee did not include any of the Ministry officials with whom we had relations prior to the invasion.

After greeting Hansenne, the Minister came towards me with a smiling face and embraced me, while uttering several words of warm welcome. As we moved towards the fleet of cars, Kuleib ushered me to accompany him with Hansenne in the same car. During the short journey to the hotel, Kuleib pointed to landmarks that showed the destruction caused by the war.

The Sheraton Hotel where we stayed was one such example. Structural damage was evident in parts of the hotel. In the operational part that housed us, electricity was provided by generators. Telephone and communication services were at the minimum. Every effort was made to make our stay comfortable yet we suffered in silence the lack of heating.

An impressive programme had been arranged for the visit, which included meetings with the Emir Sheikh Jaber Al-Ahmad Al-Sabah, the Crown Prince Sheikh Saad Al-Abdullah and the Minister of Foreign Affairs, Sheikh Sabah Al-Ahmad Al-Jaber Al-Sabah. Meetings were also scheduled with the employers' and workers' representatives.

That evening, the three of us met in Hansenne's suite, and the key topic was the special warm reception I received from the Minister. This development was an encouraging element for Hansenne to raise the issue of the conditions and future of workers, particularly Jordanians, Palestinians and Yemenis, in a more direct and forceful manner. We were struck by the evident euphoria of the Kuwaitis glorifying the liberation of their country. One aspect that raised our concern was the clear vindictive mood towards nationals whose countries did not openly condemn the invasion.

I told Hansenne that the main purpose of our visit was known to the authorities. Also, that they would be aware of what ensued in Saudi Arabia. Hence, my advice was to try and obtain assurances that no further reprisal action would be taken against any category of workers. I further suggested to the DG to lay emphasis on the technical assistance that the ILO would provide to Kuwait in its post-liberation development process.

That night, I lay in bed submerged by thoughts of the years I had spent in Kuwait and the memories of my struggle to develop my career. Snapshots of the happy and difficult moments crossed my mind. That night, I realized the wisdom of my decision to totally change the direction of my life and join the ILO.

Our first meeting, next morning, was with the Emir. We were received with all the pomp and ceremony accorded to a head of state. I had briefed Hansenne that while the meeting with the Emir was important, he should reserve detailed discussion on the major issues for the encounter with the Crown Prince and the Minister of Foreign Affairs. Our audience with Sheikh Jaber lasted for over 30 minutes. He spoke about the need for reconstruction and expressed hope to receive ILO assistance in this regard. On the issue of foreign workers, he said the policy would be to favour nationals from countries who exercised solidarity with Kuwait. Hansenne responded diplomatically by expressing the hope that all workers currently employed in the country would retain their jobs. Sheikh Jaber did not respond but it was clear from the expression on his face that he well understood the intimation.

Our next meeting was with the Crown Prince, who received us in his private palace. As we entered, the Minister of Labour introduced us to Sheikh Saad, who came towards me and embraced me saying out loud 'welcome to your country'. I was dumbfounded and saw an expression of utter amazement on Hansenne's face that simultaneously bore a smile.

Sheikh Saad showed us the remaining traces of the damage caused to his home, which was still in the process of renovation. He expressed disappointment that his home was looted by 'foreign workers to whom Kuwait had given jobs and security'.

Hansenne spoke about the injustice of penalizing innocent workers, who were non-political, and were only concerned with earning a living. He appealed to the Crown Prince to at least retain workers who had valid contracts. He expressed the hope that Kuwait would judge all workers by the same standard, once the simmering national feelings over the invasion faded away. Sheikh Saad responded by pointing to me, telling Hansenne that I was an example of those who worked in Kuwait and proved my appreciation. Addressing me directly, he said, 'Consider Kuwait as your country. You are welcome here anytime.' The meeting ended on this note. It was evident that the praise I received was a consequence of the assistance that I had provided to the Kuwaitis in processing their complaint to the Governing Body.

While naturally comforted and flattered by the compliments I received from the Crown Prince, I considered it necessary to erase any impression that I had taken sides in the Iraqi–Kuwaiti conflict. Hence, I wasted no time in pointing out to Kuleib, in the presence of Hansenne, that what I did was my duty and responsibility to a constituent in my capacity as ADG. This was done during our short journey by car to meet the Minister of Foreign Affairs.

Sheikh Sabah surprised us all by telling Hansenne that he would save him the discussion about the summary termination and deportation of foreign workers. While confirming that the state and private sector had embarked on such action during the liberation process, he gave the DG assurances that such practices would stop immediately.

He told Hansenne that the Emir and the leadership of the country fully appreciated his initiative in visiting Kuwait and that they looked forward to cooperating with the ILO in all areas, particularly the labour market and the post-war development process. Sheikh Sabah later acceded to the leadership of the country and is currently the Emir of Kuwait.

We returned to the hotel late in the afternoon in a state of disbelief. Hansenne asked me whether they would deliver on their commitment. I replied in the affirmative, while underlining that time should be given for the healing process. That night, we were guests of the Minister of Labour Kuleib for dinner, attended by senior officials of the Ministry, representatives of the workers' and employers' organizations and an impressive number of local dignitaries. Kuleib and I somehow took a liking to each other from the outset. During our meetings with the three most powerful men in the country, he participated actively in the discussions. It was clear that he commanded the respect of the leadership and that regard was given to his ideas and opinion.

The dinner provided me with the opportunity to exchange ideas with him in a conversation over a span of two hours. I was sitting on his left side and Hansenne was on his right. It was not by chance that Abdul Aziz Al-Saqer, the prominent and influential President of the Chamber of Commerce, was seated next to Hansenne.

Kuleib confided in me that extensive consultations and discussions had taken place among the leadership, prior to our arrival, on the issue of Kuwait's future policy on the foreign workers. It was clear that he played a major role in curbing the trend of retribution and penalization.

The majority of the guests, including Al-Saqer, were openly voicing their opposition to any reduction or abatement of punitive action against workers from countries that had purportedly sided against Kuwait. At one point, Kuleib turned to me with a broad smile while gesturing with his hand across the entirety of the huge table to demonstrate the mood of the population towards the issue of foreign workers. However, he assured me that Kuwait would abide by its commitment to Hansenne but that time was needed to defuse the ill feeling of the population.

The next morning, we had a lengthy meeting with Kuleib at the Ministry, during which discussions centred on issues of technical assistance to be provided by the ILO. Later in the day, we flew back to Dubai, where we had a brief meeting with Al-Jarwan, prior to embarking on the return flight to Geneva.

Our visit to Kuwait marked the beginning of a long and fruitful relation between Kuleib and myself. In fact, our cooperation served in the normalization of the relations between Kuwait and Jordan.

Thanks to Kuleib, the government of Kuwait contributed half a million dollars to an ILO project for the disabled in the West Bank. The significance of this decision and its political ramifications should be viewed with the background that for some time after the war the name Palestine was a taboo for the Kuwaitis.

Remote from publicity, the ILO action during the critical days after the Iraqi–Kuwaiti conflict was instrumental in saving the livelihood of tens, if not hundreds, of thousands of workers in the Gulf States.

On 13 June 1995, Kuleib sent me a token of our friendship in the form of a special commemorative note at the nominal value of One Kuwaiti Dinar issued by the Central Bank of Kuwait in commemoration of the Second Anniversary of Liberation Day. The following words were on the card: 'His excellency brother Shukri Al-Dajani. With my sincere appreciation and respect. Your brother Ahmed Kuleib.'

Assisting the Palestinian Authority

Following the signature of the Declaration of Principles between Israel and the PLO on 13 September 1993, I convinced Hansenne that the ILO should waste no time in offering assistance to the Palestinian Authority immediately following its move from Tunis to Gaza. A month later, I hand delivered a letter from Hansenne to Chairman Yasser Arafat, offering ILO assistance in the construction process of Gaza and the West Bank. Arafat was visibly delighted with the news. He hosted a lunch for me, which was followed by a working session, lasting several hours, during which I explained to him and his aides the areas and modalities in which ILO technical assistance could be provided.

Arafat insisted that we conclude our meeting with concrete and specific proposals. Accordingly, it was agreed, at my recommendation, that the ILO would field a high-level muldisciplinary mission to the Occupied Palestinian Territories to prepare a Programme of Action for Capacity Building for Social Development for the transition of the Territories.

Arafat requested that the mission be fielded the following month and though I explained to him the logistical difficulties of implementing such a deadline, he expressed hope that his wish would be realized. During the many hours we spent together, Arafat – whom I had met on several previous occasions – was particularly vibrant and full of optimism. He repeatedly made a point of mentioning how pleased he was that I, a Palestinian from Jerusalem, would be in charge of this major project of reconstruction. Equally so, he was praiseworthy of the Al-Dajani family and its prominent status in the Arab world.

On my departure from his residence in Tunis, he embraced me warmly while saying, 'our next meeting will be in Palestine'. To my surprise, he also handed me a letter to Hansenne, in which he confirmed his agreement for immediate ILO intervention along the lines that we had discussed. That evening, I was overwhelmed by a mixture of feelings that I had never experienced before.

In spite of my optimistic nature, the reality of events had forced me to abandon any hope of ever returning to Palestine. I was suddenly struck by a new reality that remained difficult to comprehend or digest. I had suffered throughout my life, witnessing chances of ever seeing my usurped homeland fade away with each passing month, year and decade. I needed more proof and assurance that the Oslo Accords was not another link in a chain that was so eroded that it would succumb to the least pressure. Yet the feeling of hope still brought a sense of joy and happiness in the depth of my soul.

I was proud and deeply moved that I would be responsible for a major project involving the reconstruction of a Palestinian State. This was the most rewarding task of my entire career. Most important, it would enable me to visit my country after 45 years of forced exile. The other aspect concerned the mammoth task ahead with regard to the foreseen ILO project. I realized that I had less than a month to put together a multidisciplinary team comprising 15 experts and to have the mission complete its work within four weeks, prior to the Christmas and New Year holidays.

Immediately upon my return to Geneva, I met with Hansenne, who was delighted with the outcome of my mission. He instructed all the heads of the concerned departments to give top priority to the Palestinian project – a move that assisted me considerably in overcoming the habitual red tape. I was aware that other UN agencies and organizations were scrambling to obtain Arafat's approval to engage in activities in favour of the Palestinian Authority. We needed to be on the scene, soonest, if we were to secure the financial resources for our project proposals.

The international community had committed considerable funds for the development process in Palestine, which were channelled through the World Bank, the UNDP, as well as trust funds from specific donor countries. The United Nations Secretary-General had appointed a special envoy to the Palestinian Authority territory, Mr Terje Rød-Larsen, to oversee and coordinate the implementation of the Oslo process. Rød-Larsen, who assisted in the secret talks leading to the Oslo Accords, was based in Gaza.

Thanks to the assistance of all the concerned ILO technical departments, 15 experts covering the areas of specialization needed were selected within two weeks. Simultaneously, contacts were made with the Israeli government to inform it about the mission and obtain approval for it to proceed to Palestine. The Herculean task was facilitated by a series of positive factors with regard to both the identification of the experts for the mission as well as the speedy approval given by the Israelis. The process was unprecedentedly smooth and swift.

I considered that as a good omen. With every passing day, my yearning to arrive in Palestine grew stronger. Snapshot images of sites and places in Jerusalem and Al-Bakaa Al Fouka, where we resided, featured constantly in my mind. I was so overwhelmed with emotion. At one time, I decided to abstain from any thoughts of my anticipated visit, fearing that it would not be realized.

On 5 December 1993, I set off with my team of experts to Amman, where we spent the night before heading to Jerusalem early next morning by road. The Jordanian authorities facilitated our formalities at the border, enabling us to cross the Allenby Bridge with no delay. Our convoy of cars, provided by the United Nations, arrived at the Israeli checkpoint less than a kilometre away.

Until that moment, I was fully preoccupied with anxiety about possible problems and difficulties that we might encounter with the Israeli forces. The ILO team comprised a wide range of nationalities including two Arabs and myself. We had been warned to expect possible long delays in the processing of our passports, and also that our luggage might be minutely searched despite our diplomatic status.

I was seated next to the driver in the leading car. We stopped at the barrier. An army officer approached. He asked the driver in Hebrew who we were and the purpose of our visit. Clearly, the response of the driver did not satisfy him. He came to my side addressing me in Hebrew. I replied in English, stating that I spoke no Hebrew and that we were ILO officials heading to Jerusalem. He requested to see my passport, which I handed over to him. He asked me what was my nationality, as UN passports do not indicate that. I replied that I was Jordanian of Palestinian origin. I saw him wince as he flipped through my UN laissez-passer. In the meantime, I explained to him that we had visas and approval from the Israeli government to enter the country. His response was crisp and abrupt: 'It is my commanding officer who decides and not the diplomatic or civil authority.'

He then walked away towards a small concrete building, which he entered after climbing a few steps. The driver, who was a Palestinian employee of UNDP in Jerusalem, pointed towards two large hangars in the distance with huge crowds of men, women and children queuing up outside. He explained to me that these were Palestinians who were returning home after visiting relatives in Jordan. They had to strip their clothes to the minimum. Then they had to take their luggage, one by one, to the hangar where they had to empty their contents on the floor inside the hangar for inspection by the security services. Apparently, the process would take hours for each person, and all had to stand in the open, irrespective of weather conditions.

The officer returned with a few soldiers informing us that we all had to go to the office to have our passports inspected. This we did. The process took nearly an hour during which time each of us was asked several questions, some personal and others general.

To our surprise and delight, we were then given permission to proceed on our way to Jerusalem without having our luggage checked. From that point to Jericho and then to Jerusalem, we passed through dozens of checkpoints and barriers. Though we were waved through at most of them, I sensed, as of that early stage, the ugly face of military occupation. It was late afternoon when we arrived at the Four Seasons Hotel overlooking the Mount of Olives and the old city of Jerusalem. It was only after we concluded our first meeting to draw up our plan of work, and having finished dinner, that I retired to the seclusion of my room.

I was troubled by the mixture of emotions of extreme joy and utter distress that took hold of me. I could not believe I was in Jerusalem, a lifelong wish that was realized. Simultaneously, I was already agonized by the scene of ill treatment of the Palestinians at the border crossing.

Perhaps my disillusionment stemmed from my earnest passion to return to reside one day in my homeland. Being a believer in fate and destiny, I thought the unfolding of events leading to my heading the mission could be a prelude to my retiring with my family in Jerusalem. The timing coincided with my retirement that was due in a couple of years. Before going to bed, I took a stroll on the terrace of the hotel, which provided a panoramic view of Jerusalem lit up like a pearl. I needed to convince myself that the Oslo agreement was going to endure and end the occupation. I already envisaged myself settled in Jerusalem spending the remaining years of my life in that beautiful land of my ancestors.

Arrangements had been made that all members of the ILO mission and I would meet with a delegation of high-level Israeli officials to inform them about our plan of work and discuss logistic issues. The meeting was to take place at one of the leading hotels in West Jerusalem on the morning following our arrival.

I had a restless night, finding it difficult to sleep. The pressure of the deadline for completing our mission and the unknown that awaited us on the Israeli side weighed heavily on my mind. That morning is one that will forever remain engraved in my memory. I was adorned by a feeling of confidence and strength, both physical and mental, which was unprecedented.

As the car wended its way through the traffic and military barricades between East and West Jerusalem, I was enjoying the scene of that lovely city with its dominant biblical attire. It was envisaged that I would have an exclusive meeting with the Israelis prior to the arrival of the ILO team. I was in the process of remarking the distinct contrast between the advanced development of West Jerusalem and that of the Arab East part when the car stopped.

As I emerged, I was greeted by a smiling man whose words, 'Welcome to your country Mr Al-Dajani', still ring in my ears. He was the public relations director of the Ministry of Foreign Affairs. Before we started moving towards the entrance of the hotel, he asked whether he could offer me a present, while waving a plastic folder in his hand. My response was spontaneous, perhaps with a slightly harsh tone: that as a UN official I was prohibited from accepting gifts. He quickly opened the folder from which he extracted a large piece of paper. He said it was a photocopy of a full-page article recently published in the daily Israeli newspaper *Haaretz*. He asked whether I could read Hebrew. Since I answered in the negative, he translated the heading, which said: 'The Al-Dajanis, one of the oldest families of Jerusalem'. He requested that

I accept this token gift and I agreed and thanked him for his kind gesture. As we were heading to the meeting room, he made a remark, to which I opted not to respond. He said: 'It is unfortunate that we are negotiating the peace accords with representatives of the PLO and not persons like you.'

Awaiting my arrival were half a dozen officials including an under-secretary of the Ministry of Foreign Affairs and senior officials from the Ministry of Economy and Interior. I provided them with an overview of the objectives of our mission, emphasizing that our counterpart was the Palestinian Authority. The under-secretary requested that I provide him with our plan of work and contacts. I responded that such a request should be made to the Palestinians. A brief but tense discussion ensued on this subject, during which I underlined that we hoped for and expected full cooperation from the Israelis to facilitate our work, logistically. The arrival of the ILO team was timely to defuse the exchange on this subject. The general meeting lasted for nearly one hour at the end of which agreement was reached that freedom of movement would be provided to the members of the mission in the West Bank and Gaza.

That meeting marked the beginning of the ILO's active role in Palestine. Members of the team embarked on the preparation of project proposals in close consultation with their counterparts nominated by the Palestinian Authority.

Jerusalem was witnessing a conglomeration of experts and representatives of the World Bank, the UNDP and all other United Nations agencies and organizations. In addition, numerous businessmen representing the international private sector were scrambling to obtain contracts or concessions from what was expected to become a most versatile booming economy.

Indeed the World Bank spoke of the future 'golden triangle' comprising Palestine, Jordan and Israel that would dominate the economy of the Middle East. It was this optimistic and challenging environment that further inspired the ILO team to work relentlessly to complete its mammoth task within the set deadline of two weeks.

I was savouring every hour spent with visions of peace and the establishment of a Palestinian State prevailing, that would return the existence of my country and obliterate the term 'refugee' from my mind.

Back home to Jerusalem?

For some time, I had struggled with the decision as to whether I should visit our home in Jerusalem, knowing that it had been sequestered and was occupied by Jews who had migrated from East Europe. Prompted by the positive mood for future peace, I finally decided to go. I was adamant about attempting to find the location without assistance from the driver accompanying me. I requested him to go to the YMCA building opposite the King David Hotel where I used to go with my friends on roller skates. From that point, I was directing him amidst a drastically restructured district while desperately struggling to identify some landmarks to assist me to proceed in the right direction.

I had almost despaired, when I recognized a building that was in the close vicinity of our house. A few hundred metres down the same road I told the driver to stop. I stood before our home that used to be a beautiful villa with a magnificent garden. The structure was disfigured by the construction of a second floor that massacred the original architectural design. The front of the building was draped by a huge Israeli flag. What used to be a blooming colourful garden was a barren soil covered by ashes. Apparently, the residents would burn whatever grew on the land to avoid paying taxes on gardens. I approached the garden door with the driver Ibrahim, a Palestinian Arab working for the United Nations, who spoke Hebrew very fluently. A man and a woman, who were observing us from the window of the first floor, suddenly appeared at the front door. As they were making their way towards us, they began uttering a chain of words in Hebrew. The driver engaged in a discussion with them, trying to explain that I was visiting for the first time since 1948 and wished to see my old home. While the tone of Ibrahim was calm and normal, the two persons began screaming and demonstrating an extremely aggressive attitude. In no time, no less than ten people emerged from the house carrying sticks, baseball bats and even knives, which they pointed at us in an extremely aggressive manner.

Ibrahim advised me to quickly get into the car and we sped off before they could attack us physically. Later he explained to me that they were saying no Arab had any right in Israel, that the house was theirs forever and that if I ever came again they would kill me. I was extremely shocked and stunned by the incident. While I did not wish to give undue importance to such an isolated event, I could not but question whether the political environment in Israel was conducive to implementing the Oslo peace accord.

A few days later, I went with Ibrahim to visit our family cemetery on the Mount of David.

The almost palatial house of my grandfather had been demolished and the area was used as a parking lot for the visitors and tourists who frequented the site. As we walked along the narrow lane leading to the cemetery, we came across a young man, dressed in civilian clothes, carrying an automatic rifle. He asked in Hebrew where we were going, to which Ibrahim replied, giving our destination. He told Ibrahim we could not visit because classes of the religious school next door were in session. I asked the young man if he spoke Arabic. He was a Jewish migrant from Yemen. After a lengthy discussion, I convinced him to allow me to proceed to the cemetery in his company. The door was locked. I was later informed by relatives that they had decided to take this action due to constant vandalism and desecration of the tombs.

Fortunately for me, and regrettably for the cemetery, there was an opening on one side that overlooked the graveyard. The sight was heartbreaking. The area was littered with garbage of all sorts and a massive number of empty bottles of beer.

I prayed to the memory of my mother, grandparents, uncles and aunts who are buried there and recalled the times when the sanctity of the cemetery was respected and the marble tombs, cleanliness and flowers adorned their resting souls. Irrespective of the unfortunate and regrettable episodes I encountered, I felt very much at home.

Wherever I went, when I mentioned my name, I was warmly greeted and welcomed. The name Al-Dajani had a meaning, a sense and value in my country of origin. For the first time in my adult life, I felt a real deep-rooted sense of belonging. History was unfolding the past of my family in the Holy Land and providing evidence that it very much remains an integral part of the society and country.

An unexpected event that brought the utmost joy and pride to me was when more than 20 members of the family came to the hotel one evening to welcome me back to my homeland. They were men of all ages, none of whom I knew or had met before. Some were doctors or engineers and others university professors. There were also businessmen as well as students. It was a reunion that marked me for life due to its spontaneity, sincerity and simplicity. A good part of the evening was spent in tracing the relation between us through our parents and grandparents. Only those who have tasted the bitter pill of being stateless can understand and appreciate my feeling that night when I lay in bed thinking in disbelief about what was happening. I was overwhelmed by the joy and pride of being in my country, my birthplace, my homeland.

The ILO team and I worked relentlessly to complete our assignment on time. We needed to finalize all the project proposals and submit the entire programme to the Department of Economic Affairs and Planning of the PLO for its approval on 18 January 1994. A key factor in meeting the afore-mentioned deadline was that the World Bank had requested the ILO to develop a project regarding to the ex-detainees, to the tune of US$30 million and another on public works amounting to US$45 million. These were to be presented to the Consultative Group meeting in Paris on 27 January 1994. I was caught up in a tidal wave that would either render a fatal blow to my career or carry me safely to calm waters.

For the ILO to assume its appropriate and full role in Palestine, I needed to be personally in charge of the operation. I was aware that I needed to invest a major part of my time in the operation, which involved considerable travel and extensive negotiations with the World Bank, UNDP and the donor countries. I discussed this matter in depth and detail with Hansenne. He was adamant that the ILO should play a major role in the establishment of what was foreseen as a Palestinian State. He was delighted by what had already been accomplished and undertook to provide full support to me and the Regional Office.

On Tuesday 18 January 1994, Ahmad Qurie (Abu Ala), Director-General of the Economic Affairs and Planning of the PLO and I signed the document titled, 'Capacity Building for Social Development. A Programme of Action for Transition in the Occupied Palestinian Territories'. As of that moment, I and a team of ILO experts were engaged in a marathon of discussions, negotiations and constant travel to Gaza, Washington, New York and Paris to obtain the funding for some 17 projects in favour of the Palestinian Authority to the tune of nearly US$70 million.

I should mention that Abu Ala and I developed good relations during our discussions in Tunis that went, with time, beyond the realm of official business. We took a liking to each other and remained in contact by telephone regularly. This relation was consolidated following the establishment of the Authority of Palestine and the appointment of Abu Ala as Head of the Palestinian Parliament. He was a man of considerable intelligence and charm. His role as chief negotiator at the Oslo secret talks gained him the respect of friends and foes. At a time when relations between the PLO and Jordan were lukewarm, I arranged for a secret meeting between Prince Zeid and Abu Ala at the residence of the former in Amman. During that meeting, which was restricted to the three of us, discussions focused on how to consolidate cooperation between the two entities. Abu Ala was keen on having more interaction between the Jordanian and Palestinian parliaments.

Early in 1994, a meeting was convened in Paris by the United Nations, to discuss project proposals for the Palestinians. The UN Secretary-General had nominated Mr Peter Hansen as coordinator for the UN agencies and organizations. We all met under his chairmanship to prepare for the meeting on the next day with the Palestinian delegation and that of the World Bank. Within minutes, the delegates of UNESCO and that of the UNHCR accused Hansen of bias and trying to favour some agencies. Both delegates walked out of the room and the meeting came to a chaotic and abrupt end. Hansen pleaded with me to intervene, as he observed I was friendly with the UNESCO representative, who was a Palestinian. That evening I invited them both to dinner. They made peace and Hansen was able to attend the meeting with the Palestinians on the next day without being challenged or harassed as coordinator.

Another interesting and historic happening at that meeting was that two Palestinian delegations attended with two different sets of proposals. One team represented Mr Nabil Shaat and the other Abu Ala.

Terje Rød-Larsen, the UN Secretary-General's envoy to Palestine, came to me in a state of panic. He explained to me the complexity of having two Palestinian delegations. Apparently, he was aware of that possibility prior to his departure from Jerusalem. According to Rød-Larsen, when he tried to talk by phone to Abu Ala, he accused him of siding with Shaat and slammed down the phone in his face. Ironically, Rød-Larsen and Abu Ala were among the co-authors of the Oslo agreement. Rød-Larsen knew of my good relations with Abu Ala and asked me to intervene so he could talk to him. I was very eager that the meeting in Paris should succeed and achieve its objectives. I spoke to Abu Ala by phone. No sooner had I mentioned Rød-Larsen's name that he started screaming with anger, saying it was Rød-Larsen who had encouraged Shaat to send the other team and he was the real culprit. I spent nearly half an hour on the phone calming Abu Ala and assuring him that Rød-Larsen had no part in the Shaat initiative. When the moment arrived that Abu Ala agreed to speak to Rød-Larsen, who was standing next to me all the time, I handed the phone over to him and the differences between the two key players on the Palestinian scene were resolved. The mood at the meeting on the next day was tense and chaotic. Each of the Palestinian delegations presented different proposals. The UN representatives spoke while Hansen played the role of observer rather than coordinator. Rød-Larsen remained silent to avoid problems upon his return to Gaza. The World Bank representatives thanked all present and terminated the meeting a day earlier than scheduled 'to give time for further consultations and coordination among all parties concerned.'

The events that occurred in Paris on the occasion of that meeting convinced me more than ever before of the value of maintaining good relations and contacts with persons of authority and status. In fact, I became the pivotal point at that meeting. Both Hansen and Rød-Larsen were rescued by my interventions and I even assisted in defusing the tension between the two opposing Palestinian delegations due to my good relations with Abu Ala and Shaat.

It was evident that the process of establishing the Palestinian Authority was going through teething problems both at the national and international levels and that the process required cohesion, patience and understanding among the key players.

The following months witnessed a series of meetings by the World Bank organized in Washington and Paris. This was the period that heralded the beginning of concrete commitments by donor countries, which enabled the ILO to launch its projects. During the period 1994 to 1997, ILO projects in the West Bank and Gaza were established in multiple areas and their positive impact was recognized by the recipient as well as donor countries.

The ILO blueprint for Capacity Building for Social Development was approved and adopted in its entirety with projects including the establishment of a Ministry of Labour, labour laws, the rehabilitation of ex-detainees, setting up a department of statistics, vocational training and rehabilitation and assistance to employers' and workers' organizations, among other things.

More than US$50 million had been raised for the projects, which placed the ILO as the leading UN organization operating in the newly established Palestinian entity.

In fact, the Programme for Palestine became one of the largest for the ILO. Hansenne was so delighted with the outcome, he decided to visit Palestine in 1995.

His programme included meetings with Israeli dignitaries as well as Palestinians, headed by Arafat. It was on that occasion that I visited the Knesset, meeting some of its members. We spent one night at the King David Hotel. This brought to my mind the sad memories of the day it was blown up in 1948 by Israeli militants, rocking our house in Jerusalem, and killing dozens of British officers and soldiers, and wounding others in large numbers.

I was delighted by Hansenne's visit. I wanted him to have first-hand knowledge and experience the conditions of Palestinians living under occupation. While negotiations were ongoing regarding the implementation of the peace accords, no easing or improvements were evident in the restrictions imposed by the Israelis.

One day, I arrived at the checkpoint to enter Gaza where I was scheduled to have a meeting with Arafat and the Minister of Labour. While our driver Ibrahim headed with my UN laissez-passer to the kiosk housing the Israeli soldiers, I spotted Samir Ghawshah, the Minister of Labour, sitting in his car. I descended from the UN vehicle and went to greet him. He informed me he had been waiting for almost one hour for permission to proceed. Clearly uneasy and uncomfortable with the deliberate delay, he indicated that it was habitual for Palestinian government officials to be treated in this manner. Within minutes, Ibrahim returned having obtained clearance for us to proceed. Ghawshah arrived at the meeting with Arafat more than one hour later.

Hansenne was visibly shaken by many of the measures taken by Israel with regard to the movement and treatment of the Palestinian population.

His meeting with Arafat was an event which he described as 'historic'. Arafat hosted a lunch for us in the presence of several cabinet ministers. On that occasion, the Minister of Labour and I signed a document for a project on vocational training to be implemented by the ILO. Upon our departure, Arafat was adamant about escorting Hansenne to the car awaiting us. He was full of thanks and praise to the ILO for its assistance, which he described as 'vital to the state of Palestine'.

In December of each year, it is customary that the Director-General addresses the staff at a huge gathering to provide a review of the key events that occurred and outline future plans and aspirations. Hansenne's speech on 14 December 1995 contained the following paragraph:

> After my return from a mission in Israel and the Occupied Territories, I could also talk to you about the needs and problems of the Palestinians. This is an immense task and an enormous responsibility for the International Labour Organization, practically the only United Nations institution present on the spot with projects based on real situations. Why? Because Mr Al-Dajani and his team have managed to mobilize external donors to which undoubtedly none of us would have given thought. We shall now be able to launch a series of projects because we have been able to develop interesting ideas which have caught the imagination of donors.

The success story of the ILO programme for Palestine interested the Chairman of the Governing Body at the time. Yvon Chotard, who was the government representative of France, had distinguished himself as an active and influential member for many years before being elected as Chairman. He was the only delegate to be elected twice to the post of Chairman of the Governing Body for the periods 1991–92 and 1995–96.

Chotard was noted for his impressive physical appearance – exceeding two metres in height – his gait and his loud husky voice.

He contacted me one day expressing his desire to visit Palestine to witness, at first hand, the ILO's ongoing activities.

I was delighted by the request as it could lead to much needed financial support from the ILO constituents and, more importantly, from France and the European Union to the ILO programme in favour of the Palestinians. Within weeks, Chotard and I visited the West Bank and

Gaza. He was warmly welcomed by Arafat and many of the members of the Palestinian leadership. He showed deep and keen interest in all the ILO activities and openly expressed abhorrence to the occupation and the 'inhuman' conditions under which the Palestinians lived.

Immediately upon his return, he was instrumental in increasing the ILO regular budget financial contribution to the activities in Palestine and obtained funding for the programme from the European Union.

Chotard remained an ardent supporter of the ILO projects and the Regional Office for Arab States until he passed away in 1998.

ILO projects launched in the 1990s provided the backbone to the Palestinian Authority in the areas of specialization of the Organization. Many of the projects were successfully completed, while others remain ongoing.

Other key contacts in Palestine

I deem it necessary to recount the story of the contacts and relations I established during the four years I was responsible for ILO activities in Palestine. My relations with Abu Ala, which started in Tunis, developed further when the PLO returned to Palestine, following the Oslo Accords. I found in Abu Ala a counterpart who was a workaholic with a strong desire to overcome red tape and obtain results. We were in close contact, mostly by telephone. He was an asset at all times, providing valuable assistance and advice and sincere friendship.

Terje Rød-Larsen and I became close friends. We had numerous things in common and very much enjoyed each other's company. We worked very closely together in a manner that was complementary to each other. I assisted him to strengthen and consolidate his relations with the Palestinians, while he assisted me in supporting and promoting our projects. He came several times to Geneva and met Hansenne on one occasion. He was extremely well connected on the Israeli side, particularly with the late Shimon Peres, with whom he often spoke by telephone, while I was in his company.

It was Rød-Larsen who introduced me to Suha Arafat, the wife of Yasser Arafat, at a cocktail reception he was hosting in Gaza. She expressed deep interest in the work that the ILO was undertaking and was particularly keen on our programme for combating child labour. That evening marked the beginning of a close friendship between us. She is an extremely intelligent person, who was fully aware of the negative elements that were infiltrating the leadership. In time, I became her confidant. She would reveal to me her fears and concerns about some aides who surrounded her husband. I respected her sense of judgement, her strength of character and ability to survive in an environment full of intrigue and scheming.

On my last mission to Palestine prior to my retirement, I was accompanied by my wife and children Shireen and Zaki, as this was the only possibility for them to see their country. Suha invited us to lunch and was very proud to present her baby daughter to my wife. We spent a whole afternoon with her. My wife had complimented her on a colourful hand-embroidered jacket she was wearing, a masterpiece of Palestinian handicraft. As we were departing, Suha handed over to my wife a packet containing the jacket, which she offered her as a gift.

Though I had met Arafat several times in Lebanon, Tunis and Geneva, my relations with him became close as the ILO Palestinian programme became operational, following the PLO move to Gaza. I would meet with him at least once a month, sometimes at midnight. He was a charmer. Often when I walked into his office, he would be sitting at the head of a long table with dozens of files covering its surface. Once I ventured to ask him why he did not request someone to assist him in dealing with the endless chain of files. With a big smile adorning his face, he told me they contained cheques of salaries and other dues to officials of all ranks, from ministers to messenger boys. 'Only I have the right and authority to sign these cheques. This is how I control everybody.' With that remark, he roared with laughter, telling me I merited the highest decoration for all the work and assistance I was providing to the Palestinians.

He always had his door open for me and welcomed me with enthusiasm and warmth. With time, whenever I went to Gaza to meet Arafat, Suha would invite me to lunch at their home. Arafat used to quip that I preferred to have lunch with his wife, to which I always responded with a smile. He often remarked that he was aware his wife was complaining to me about some bad elements surrounding him. He would then laugh, indicating that it was her concern for his safety that prompted her to react that way.

While the ILO's projects were advancing satisfactorily and continuously expanding, negotiations between the Palestinians and Israelis to implement the Oslo Accords were stagnant. Each party blamed the other for the protraction and conditions in the occupied West Bank and Gaza were rapidly deteriorating.

I wish to recount an event that is indicative of the difficult conditions which the Palestinian Authority has encountered at certain junctures of its existence.

In February 2002, I was at Geneva airport in the process of checking-in for my flight to London. I was embarking on a three-day visit to meet Prince Zeid, who had arrived the day before. Ghazi was also in London and the three of us were very much looking forward to our get-together.

I felt a tap on my shoulder and turning around found Ambassador Nabil Ramlawi, the Head of the Permanent Mission of Palestine to the United Nations in Geneva. He told me he was planning to contact me the following day to discuss an urgent problem.

He confided in me that the Authority had been encountering serious financial problems during the past year. He revealed to me that the rent for the mission's office premises had not been paid for over a year and that an eviction order had been issued. Ramlawi asked whether any of my friends might be able and interested in providing a donation to resolve the rental crisis he was facing. My response was that I would sound out possible donors but that the chances of success were very limited.

That evening I had dinner with Prince Zeid, Ghazi and another close Old Victorian friend. During the course of the evening, I mentioned my encounter with Ramlawi and his request for financial assistance. The friend asked about the amount required. When I gave him the figure, which was quite substantial, he told me he would arrange for payment, through me, on condition that he remained anonymous. Upon my return to Geneva, I contacted Ramlawi and arranged for payment of the amount. A few weeks later, I received an official letter from him thanking me and the anonymous donor for his generous contribution.

Each time I visited Palestine, within a span of a few months, I witnessed more stringent rules being applied by the Israelis and more frustration on the side of the Palestinians. The optimism of Arafat, Abu Ala and other Palestinian high-ranking officials was giving way to doubt and gradual pessimism. They openly expressed their inability to forge ahead with the implementation of the peace plan. According to Abu Ala, who was a key player in the Oslo talks, the Israelis were reneging on major parts of the agreement. He said they wished to renegotiate each paragraph claiming that their interpretation of the text differed from that of the Palestinians.

With each passing day, I saw my dream of residing in Palestine after my imminent retirement dwindling away. I had never mentioned that dream either to my wife or to any member of my family, fearing it may not be realized. For a period of time, I lived a situation of hoping against hope. I was resisting the harsh reality developing before me with disbelief.

Palestinians and Israelis were deadlocked in their negotiations. Terje Rød-Larsen confided in me that the situation was grave and there was little hope of resolving the 'major differences' that existed between the two parties. Hopes of realizing the 'golden triangle' were rapidly fading away and a sombre political and economic mood dawned on the entire region. The enthusiasm of key players and donor countries vanished. Raising funds became problematic as the entire world seemed to turn its back on the dream of establishing a Palestinian State. In the process, my life-long aspiration to return to my homeland and be buried, one day, next to my mother and ancestors vanished through the gate of no-return.

8

History in the Making Between the ILO and the Gulf States

As already noted, a predominant problem in Western Asia during my term in office as Director and later as Assistant Director-General for the Arab States concerned the non-existence of trade unions or freedom of association in the Gulf States (with the exception of the State of Kuwait). An extremely hostile environment existed between the International Confederation of Arab Trade Unions (ICATU) and the governments of the Gulf States. The ICATU regularly sent complaints to the ILO about the suppression of trade union rights and freedoms in the Gulf countries, particularly in Saudi Arabia. Meetings convened by the ILO and the Arab Labour Organization (ALO) witnessed scenes of serious confrontations between representatives of the ICATU and the concerned governments.

Despite some unofficial meetings among the adversaries, on the occasion of the convening of the annual International Labour Conference and the Arab Labour Conference, no progress was achieved until the early 1990s. This historic breakthrough was a result of meticulous planning on my part over a long period of time. While fully acknowledging the complexity and considerable sensitivity of the issue, I was determined to exert every effort to resolve that deadlock. To continue turning a blind eye to this major problem would neither serve the interests of the ILO nor the Arab States. It was inconceivable and unacceptable to allow such conflict, which concerned the core of ILO standards, to persist with all its negative and unwholesome consequences on the environment among the Arab tripartite constituents at the national, regional and international levels.

It is worth noting that during the 1970s and 1980s, the ILO was regarded with great suspicion by the Gulf States. The organization was looked upon as a 'leftist or socialist' entity. The impression among the leadership in the Gulf States was that it was a body representing workers and their interests, in many ways targeting their national systems. In reality, the decision of the Gulf countries, led by Saudi Arabia, to join the ILO was a move intended to provide them with a certain amount of immunity against the constant and harsh attacks by the ICATU and the International Confederation of Free Trade Unions (ICFTU). In a way, they were playing the role of an ostrich, not realizing that such a move would only provide them with short-term protection. The Gulf States, however, did not obtain membership in a clandestine manner. The ILO was fully aware of their lack of full credentials. Rather than refuse their membership, until such time that they fully qualified, the Organization decided to take them on board, in order to assist these states to achieve the required standards.

It was within this context that one had to gradually allay fears and project the tripartite structure of the Organization, its function and objectives in a palatable manner. After several years of careful analyses and assessment of the realities on the ground and following the occurrence of certain major developments, I was encouraged to delve into this intricate affair.

Towards tripartism in the Gulf

On 29 April 1992, the Norwegian Foreign Minister, Mr Stoltenberg, announced that his government was financing a project for the ICFTU, to the amount of 15 million Belgian francs, to address the 'problem of the non-existence of the most basic trade union rights in many Middle Eastern Countries'.

The project clearly stipulated that contacts would be made with the ICATU to acquaint it with the objectives of the operation and solicit its full cooperation in the anticipated activities. It was clear that the project primarily targeted the Gulf States and that if these countries did not mend their fences with ICATU they would become extremely vulnerable to attack, both at the regional and international levels.

The ICATU had a new secretary-general in the person of Hassan Jamam, a noted Algerian trade unionist. Hassan and I established good work relations and, with time, he confided in me that he was keen and anxious to establish serious and constructive dialogue with the Gulf States. He requested me to assist in opening channels with one or two of the Gulf Ministers of Labour for this purpose.

I had already formulated a regular annual programme of activities with the ICATU, with financing from the ILO. The programme was subject to the condition that the ICATU would not attack the Gulf States in events or activities funded by the regional office. Simultaneously, I had cultivated excellent relations with the Minister of Labour of Saudi Arabia, Sheikh Mohamed Al-Fayez and the UAE Minister of Labour, Saif Al-Jarwan. These two high-ranking officials were playing a lead role among the Ministers of the Gulf Cooperation Council. Both Ministers had noted with great satisfaction the more moderate attitude of the ICATU towards them, ever since my cooperation arrangements with Jamam were enforced.

After several months of being mediator between the two parties, and having reached agreement on certain points for discussions, I arranged a meeting between Sheikh Al-Fayez and Hassan Jamam. I did not wish to attend or to be party to the encounter, yet I was obliged to do so as both made my presence a condition.

I had prepared the ground sufficiently that both officials immediately embarked on a constructive dialogue from the very outset of the encounter. Sheikh Al-Fayez explained that each Gulf State had its unique situation and that it was paramount for the ICATU not to make demands for improvement at the Gulf Cooperation Council level, but rather begin with the state that was most conducive to commence change. In this regard, he proposed that a meeting between the Minister of Labour of the United Arab Emirates and Jamam be held soon to discuss measures for cooperation in the near future. Within weeks, Jamam received an official invitation from Al-Jahwan to visit the Emirates.

Jamam's visit to the UAE marked a turning point in the history between ICATU and the Gulf States. As of that moment contacts between Sheikh

Al-Fayez, Al-Jarwan, Jamam and myself were continuous, almost on a weekly basis.

The words trade union were taboo and a stumbling block in the negotiations. Following the saying 'what's in a name', I proposed the establishment initially of 'coordination committees' among professional associations that would be a first step to prepare the ground for forming workers' organizations. Al-Jarwan was far-sighted and was aware of the need for change, in view of the rapid economic development in his country and the influx of hundreds of thousands of migrant workers of all nationalities. He worked with Jamam with all sincerity and transparency, always indicating the limitations of his mandate within the prevailing conditions. In his turn, Jamam appreciated Al-Jarwan's efforts. He demonstrated patience and understanding but constantly recalled his own responsibilities as Secretary-General and his obligations towards the ICATU for concrete measures to be taken.

Over time, my role became that of a moderator and peacemaker between the two officials, who became my close friends and confidants. Whenever matters stumbled, one or the other of the two would contact me to intervene. Sheikh Al-Fayez was fully briefed on all progress – or lack thereof. The four of us worked as a team and through our initiative and cooperation, the foundation was laid for the labour movement in the Gulf States to see the light at the end of the tunnel.

In February 1996, it was the turn of the Asia and Pacific Region (ASPAG), to which Western Asia belongs, to preside over the ILC. The group nominated Al-Jarwan in appreciation of the active role he was playing in the entire region. He had distinguished himself at the ILO and other meetings he attended, over a span of several years.

It was one morning during the last week of February that Mrs Sarfati, Hansenne's secretary, phoned me, requesting that I go immediately to meet the Director-General. Her voice echoed a note of extreme urgency and even a degree of panic. Upon my arrival, she was waiting in the corridor in front of Hansenne's office with an uncustomary look of anxiety on her face. She was an extremely seasoned and efficient person, who was noted for her calm and composed attitude. So this was unusual, to say the least.

She opened the door and I saw Hansenne in an almost hysterical state. While I was in the process of taking a seat, he told me he had just finished a meeting with 'Bill' Jordan, the Secretary-General of the ICFTU, and with Lord 'Bill' Brett, the Workers' spokesman at the ILO Governing Body. They had informed him that the Workers' group would boycott the International Labour Conference if Al-Jarwan were to preside. They indicated that the Workers' group would never accept a President of an ILC who came from a country that did not recognize trade unions. Hansenne told me that I should dissuade the Minister from accepting this honour to avoid the 'catastrophic consequences'.

This was the only time in my experience that he spoke continuously for nearly 20 minutes, detailing his discussions with workers' representatives and the seriousness of their position. It was only when he ran out of steam and I felt he had off-loaded his dilemma that I explained to him that Al-Jarwan was the candidate of ASPAG and not West Asia. Accordingly, it was up to the group, at large, to approach the Minister and not me.

I could see frustration and anger written all over Hansenne's face as a reaction to my remark. I quickly added that I would need one week to handle this matter in a manner that would avert a crisis. To my utter shock and surprise, he responded by agreeing to my request without asking any question about the action I intended to undertake. As I was leaving his office, he casually said that he relied on me to resolve the problem.

I immediately went to see Heribert Maier, the Deputy Director-General, who was a nominee of the Workers' group. Harry and I had very close work relations and had developed a strong personal friendship. I informed Harry about my meeting with Hansenne and the threat made to him by the Workers' group to boycott the ILC. I wished to know from him whether the workers would be flexible, if I succeeded in having the UAE ratify a couple of ILO Conventions before the Conference. This was a proposition which I was in no way certain would meet the approval of Al-Jarwan. Furthermore, the time factor for the ratification process was almost impossible to meet. Harry agreed that my idea was the 'only' hope to solve the deadlock. He said he would sound out the Workers about the proposal but expressed a certain amount of scepticism 'considering the complexity of the issue'.

I planned to leave next day for the Emirates to meet Al-Jarwan. I had spoken to him on the telephone advising him that we needed to meet urgently to discuss some 'complications' relating to his candidature to preside over the forthcoming ILC. I also made arrangements to meet the

ICFTU Director in Geneva, Guy Ryder, together with Harry immediately upon my return on 8 March.

Late that evening, I telephoned Jamam in Damascus and informed him about the Workers' message to Hansenne. I requested that he send a letter immediately to Lord Brett, expressing the ICATU's full support for Al-Jarwan's candidature. I underlined that his communication should highlight Al-Jarwan's cooperation with ICATU over recent years and his constructive and praiseworthy efforts to promote dialogue between the ICATU and the Gulf States as a first step towards the recognition of trade union rights in the future.

During my almost seven-hour flight on the next day from Geneva to Dubai, I was engrossed by the conglomerate of problems facing me. One of my major concerns was that Al-Jarwan's reaction would simply be to opt out. He was a self-made man coming from a modest background. He gained the respect of the country's leaders through his hard work, loyalty and dedication. Often he worked until the early hours of the morning, almost daily commuting several hundred kilometres between the Ministry's offices in Dubai and Abu Dhabi and his residence in Al-Fujairah. Modesty was among his finest qualities. His character was contrary to involvement in conflicts, let alone being the cause of one.

It was not a secret that Labour Ministers in some of the Gulf States were critical of Al-Fayez and Al-Jarwan for opening this dialogue with the ICATU. They were of the opinion that this would weaken their position and embolden attacks against them by both the ICFTU and ICATU. The withdrawal of Al-Jarwan's candidature would confirm the validity of their viewpoint and constitute a severe blow to the process of the cooperation we had established over a number of years. My dilemma had many facets. It was probable that Al-Jarwan would decide to withdraw his candidature. There was a possibility that he would not be willing, or able, to adopt my proposal regarding the ratification of the Conventions. To add to the complexity of the situation, I could provide no guarantee at that stage to Al-Jarwan that the Workers' group would agree to such an arrangement.

There was too much at stake for me and by the time I landed in Dubai, I was determined to find an equitable solution to satisfy all parties concerned. I was met at the airport by the Under-Secretary, Mohammed Suweidi. It was late in the evening and we drove directly to the Ministry of

Labour in Dubai. Al-Jarwan met me with his customary warm welcome and gave instructions that we were to be left alone without interruption.

I wasted no time in informing him in detail about what had occurred in Geneva regarding his candidature. I observed a clear expression of concern on his face. Before he was able to react, I followed by explaining to him my proposal regarding the Conventions, adding that I hoped to obtain the Workers' agreement. The one major point I emphasized was that the problem was in no way linked to him as a person but to the fact that trade unions were not recognized in the UAE.

As I had anticipated, Al-Jarwan's first reaction was to indicate his preference to withdraw and not be the cause of a crisis for the ILO and the Asia and Pacific Group. He then asked me directly what I would recommend for him to do.

My reply was brief and to the point. I reminded him that he was the candidate of the largest region in the ILO and that it would not be appropriate nor diplomatic if he unilaterally decided to withdraw. I sincerely believed he fully merited this honour, all the more for being a pivotal figure in having the courage and will to establish dialogue with the ICATU, in spite of harsh criticism from many of his colleagues in the Gulf States. I told him he should maintain his candidature and that I would do my best to solve the problem.

Al-Jarwan responded with a statement that will remain vividly in my memory: 'I trust you and your judgement, my dear friend, let us go ahead with the will of God.' He then called in Under-Secretary Suweidi and his special adviser for the ILO and International Affairs, Yusif Ja'afar. We stayed discussing in detail into the night what needed to be done and outlined the plan of action required. First and foremost was Al-Jarwan's mission to sound out the Prime Minister regarding the key issue of the ratification. He pointed out that this would eventually require approval of the cabinet and that of the head of state.

I remained in the Emirates to await the initial response of the Prime Minister. To my utmost joy and surprise, on the third day, Al-Jarwan informed me that he had a green light from the Prime Minister and that the proposal would be submitted to the cabinet within a week. After extensive in-house discussions at the ministry and consultations between Al-Jarwan and the Prime Minister, it was decided that the two Conventions for ratification would be the Abolition of Forced

Labour Convention (No. 105) and the Equal Remuneration Convention (No. 100). I immediately informed Harry Maier about this positive development so he could follow up and prepare the ground for our imminent meeting with Guy Ryder.

I returned to Geneva after five days of absence to find a letter from Lord Brett marked 'Private and Confidential' and another marked 'Strictly Personal' from Yvon Chotard, who was Chairman of the Governing Body at the time. The letter from Lord Brett referred to my anticipated meeting with Guy Ryder. He specified the points of contention the Workers' group had with Al-Jarwan's candidature. He made it clear that opposition was not to Al-Jarwan in person, but to what he represented. He appealed to me to use my personal good relations with Al-Jarwan to persuade him 'to delay the candidacy of the UAE for another year.' Lord Brett also indicated that the ICFTU had canvassed the opinion of its Arab affiliates, who shared its position on the issue in hand.

The note from Chotard was accompanied by a clipping of an article published on 26 February 1996, in the French magazine *Elle*. This concerned a meeting held in Abu Dhabi between Mrs Marie-Claire Mendès-France – the widow of a former prime minister and a leading journalist in her own right – and Mrs Sarah Balabagan. Sarah, a young Filipina, had been sentenced to death by a UAE court for assassinating her employer, whom she claimed had been raping her consistently over a long period of time. Mrs Mendès-France was the Chairperson of a Committee that was created to 'Save Sarah'. Chotard underlined his anxiety over this matter, while drawing attention to the fact that the President of France, Jacques Chirac, was named as the guest of honour at the forthcoming ILC.

In addition to all these complications, a complaint had been filed against the UAE for abuse of child labour, by using adolescent boys as jockeys in camel racing. I must admit there were moments when I felt as if I were caught in a vicious circle of events and circumstances that seemed endless. Each time I appeared to solve a problem, a new one arose. On the positive side, I found in my confidential in-tray a copy of a communication that Hassan Jamam had sent, on behalf of the ICATU, to Lord Brett confirming support of his Confederation and its affiliates to the candidature of Al-Jarwan.

I was delighted to note that the text of the communication was almost identical to what I had suggested. This development was of immense importance to my negotiating power with the ICFTU. In fact, it meant that there would be a rift among the Workers' representatives if the ICFTU maintained its current position.

My determination to have Al-Jarwan preside over the ILC never wavered. It was not only that he had pioneered the initiative to interact with the ICATU, hence creating a spearhead for the trade union movement in the Gulf States, but also to ensure continuity and consolidation of the hard work that I had invested over several years to achieve this end.

On 8 March, I met in the morning with Maier to learn about developments during my absence and to prepare for our meeting with Ryder for lunch. Maier's reaction to the communications from Lord Brett and Chotard was garnished with pessimism. He was not sure if the ICFTU would change its position in exchange for the ratification of the two Conventions that I had managed to organize. He was unaware, up to that moment in time, of the commitment by the ICATU to support Al-Jarwan. The minute I showed him a copy of the communication from Jamam, he stared at me with an expression of disbelief adorning his face. His words remain ringing in my ears, 'You are a wizard. How on earth did you manage to do this?' He agreed with me that this turn of events considerably weakened the ICFTU's position and that a compromise solution might be found.

I had met Ryder, in passing, on several occasions before, but never had the opportunity to get to know him professionally. Maier had spoken highly of him, and I had considerable respect for his judgement and evaluation of people. When we arrived at the restaurant, Ryder was already there. He greeted us warmly and the atmosphere was relaxed and friendly.

I informed Ryder, in some detail, about my mission to the UAE and about the government's decision to ratify two Conventions. I also gave a brief historic background of events during the recent years, vis-à-vis the trade union movements in the Gulf States, and the pivotal role of Al-Jarwan. Within the first 15 minutes of our meeting, it was clear that Ryder was a seasoned and far-sighted negotiator. He had obviously been informed about the ICATU's support to Al-Jarwan but made no reference to it. Instead, he indicated his desire to reach a solution that would safeguard the interests of the ICFTU and the ILO in the medium- and long-term. Contrary to my nature, I took a liking to Ryder in a relatively short time. I was impressed by his humility, sincerity and constructive attitude.

By the time we finished lunch, an agreement was reached that Al-Jarwan would preside at the ILC in June. We acknowledged that considerable work needed to be done, and envisaged that we would meet regularly to finalize all pending matters. I mentioned to Ryder the contents of the communication I received from Chotard and the complaint filed against the UAE on child labour and it was agreed that we would cooperate in handling both issues.

Returning to the office late in the afternoon, Maier and I headed straight to Hansenne's office to inform him about the outcome of our meeting with Ryder. I do not exaggerate if I say that Hansenne almost fell out of his chair when I transmitted to him the good news of the ICFTU's agreement to Al-Jarwan's candidacy. In reality, I had communicated little information about developments to Hansenne, due to the rapid evolution of events and the lack of substantive results.

In the evening, I transmitted the good news to Al-Jarwan, urging him to ensure that the necessary measures were taken to implement the ratification process as promised. I also brought to his attention the delicate and sensitive case of 'Sarah', the young Filipina in prison. I reiterated to him Chotard's appeal to me, particularly as President Chirac was the ILC guest of honour. I also warned Al-Jarwan that he should have a satisfactory response to the claim of child labour practices in the UAE, in order to avoid open criticism and embarrassment. While I was confident he would deliver on the issue of the ratifications, I had serious doubts he could intervene in the case of 'Sarah'.

The following day, I had a lengthy meeting with Lord Brett, who expressed his delight about the compromise reached. He and I had a very special relationship based on common values and professional and mutual respect. Thanks to this relationship, over a period of many years, we managed to resolve umpteen problems and developed a friendship that endured until he passed away on 29 March 2012.

Immediately after meeting Lord Brett, I requested an appointment with Chotard, who was in Geneva to preside over the March Governing Body session. Within minutes, his secretary contacted me to say he wished to invite me to dinner that night at his hotel, the Bristol. When I arrived at

8pm, he was waiting for me in the dining room where I was met with a very warm reception. I was certain he had been fully briefed by Hansenne and Lord Brett about the arrangements reached with the Workers' group. Chotard's concern, however, related more to the French aspect specified in his communication to me.

He was a connoisseur of wine and was always pleased to give a detailed history of the wine he chose. Having finished the ceremonial act of tasting the wine, his first words were to congratulate me for the 'great job' I did in resolving the crisis with the Workers. He showed great interest in knowing the details about my discussions with Al-Jarwan and Ryder. He clearly was pleased that we had overcome that major obstacle that was confronting the ILC.

Chotard then asked what I had done about the case of 'Sarah' and whether I had discussed the matter with Al-Jarwan. I responded in the affirmative to his question. Being conscious of the highly sensitive issue in hand, I was determined to be direct and precise, leaving no room for ambiguity or misconception. I repeated to him Al-Jarwan's words to me that the case of Sarah was in the hands of the judiciary, that it had made a considerable social stir in the country and that the only thing he could do was to mention to the Prime Minister the contents of Chotard's communication to me. I was not certain how Chotard would react to my statement. He lifted his glass, saying, 'I thank you my friend, and I drink to your good health.'

Our conversation for the rest of the evening touched on several matters of general interest but nothing about the ILC. While bidding me farewell at the hotel door, Chotard said to me, 'You wield more influence than anyone can imagine. The ILO is lucky to have you.' While I certainly welcomed the compliment, I was intrigued and mystified by what Chotard meant by that remark.

With each passing week, Al-Jarwan and his team became more demanding for information regarding the minutest details on the functions and responsibilities of the President. It was evident that the leadership of the UAE, and possibly the Gulf States, became conscious of the importance of that honour and the benefits as well as the consequences it entailed. Perhaps it is inappropriate that I use such terminology but I consider it the most apt description to say that I felt like the father of the bride at the opening session of the Conference!

By the time the initial ceremony was over, I was certain that my mission had been well accomplished. Al-Jarwan conducted the proceedings in an admirable manner. The tripartite constituents were vocal about their appreciation of his humility and wisdom and the manner in which he dealt with problems that arose.

President Chirac's visit constituted a very special and important event for Al-Jarwan. He was to present the French President with a personal gift from the Ruler of the UAE, Sheikh Zayed bin Sultan Al-Nahyan, in the form of a handmade replica, in gold, of an ancient site in Abu Dhabi.

The meeting took place after President Chirac had delivered his speech in plenary. Al-Jarwan wanted me to be the interpreter during the encounter. I declined, explaining that my command of the French language was not up to the required standard. I did, however, agree to accompany him throughout the meeting, which lasted for nearly 15 minutes. I will forever recall the evident delight on Chirac's face when the gift was unveiled. His appreciation was publicly demonstrated as he repeatedly instructed his aide to personally carry the box on the return flight to Paris and not put it with the luggage.

The Conference ended successfully without any setback or problem. The minute Al-Jarwan declared the end of the session, Lord Brett was the first person to mount the podium and congratulate Al-Jarwan for his 'outstanding presidency'. That evening we had dinner at the Hotel Intercontinental where Al-Jarwan was staying. As we were leaving the restaurant, he asked if I could accompany him to his suite. He dismissed all the officials, saying he wished to have a private meeting with me. In his customary quiet manner, he said he had very important information that he wished to share with me.

The first was that the government intended to ban the system of adolescent jockeys and introduce some form of dummies instead. The second was that he 'believed' that Sarah, the Filipina, may receive a 'Presidential Reprieve' in the not too distant future and be sent back to her country.

His face lit up with a smile and he assured he would continue to follow up on both cases. I was utterly dumbfounded by what I heard. Admittedly, my relation with Al-Jarwan was intimate and based on mutual trust and respect but I was surprised he would reveal possible future developments about Sarah. Al-Jarwan had delivered on his commitment when the UAE ratified two ILO Conventions within the agreed time-frame. The government also prohibited the system of using minors as 'jockeys' for camel races.

Most importantly, Sarah did receive the 'Presidential Reprieve' and was repatriated to the Philippines. In fact, it was Chotard who phoned from Paris to break the news to me. In high praise, he reminded me of his parting words the night we dined together at the Bristol, regarding 'wielding power'.

I assured him he was giving me more credit than I deserved, that I was merely a broker who transmitted his message to Al-Jarwan. It was a situation where events and circumstances, both at the national and international levels, had been conducive to an equitable resolution. Hence, it was fate and destiny that prevailed. Chotard remained convinced that my handling of the issue comprised a crucial element.

The Gulf countries shed the ostrich attitude

The 1996 International Labour Conference marked a historic landmark in the relations between the Gulf States and the ILO. As of that time, these countries had shed their ostrich attitudes. They realized that their interest was better served by openly interacting with the ILO and participating in its programmes and activities. In fact, Al-Jarwan's presidency was tantamount to giving a green light to the Gulf countries to fully engage as ILO member states. Thanks to Ministers Al-Jarwan and Al-Fayez, as well as Jamam of the ICATU and the ILO Regional Office for the Arab States, the Gulf States currently benefit from ILO technical assistance programmes in multiple areas. They are members of the Governing Body. Their delegations, which also include women, participate actively at the ILC as well as regional and sub-regional conferences and meetings organized by the ILO. Most importantly, they are in the process of acknowledging the imperative eventuality of granting trade union rights and freedoms. However, in this regard, progress continues to differ from state to state as was foreseen and predicted at the outset of negotiations between Al-Fayez Al-Jarwan, Jamam and myself.

Al-Fayez became Saudi Minister of Civil Service in 1999, when that Ministry was created, and still holds that post at the time of writing. Al-Jarwan was involved in a dramatic car accident in the Emirates. He miraculously escaped death but was paralysed and he remains sadly confined to a wheelchair.

Harry Maier retired, to return to his country home near Graz in Austria. I visited him on two occasions and was overwhelmed by the warmth of his reception and hospitality. An ardent horse rider who loved nature, he was ever so popular in his 'village', where inhabitants nicknamed him 'President'. Harry died on 6 November 2007 and his departure was a considerable loss to all who knew him.

Hassan Jamam passed away as a result of a heart attack. Many attribute his sudden and early departure to his profound remorse over the tragic conditions befalling the Arab world as of the 1990s, and their consequential domino effect in fragmenting the ICATU and the trade union movement as a whole.

Guy Ryder joined the ILO in 1999 as Chief of Cabinet of Director-General Juan Somavía, who succeeded Hansenne. In 2002, he returned to the ICFTU to occupy the post of Secretary-General and subsequently of its successor body the ITUC. He returned to the ILO as Executive Director for Standards in 2010, until he was elected Director-General of the ILO in 2012. Guy was re-elected for a second term of five years in October 2016.

It is worth noting that Guy made history, being the first ever Director-General to be elected from the Workers' ranks. Until his appointment, all nine previous heads of the ILO were nominees from governments. A very large segment of ILO constituents believed Guy's candidature would never see light, because of his Workers' background. I was among those who, from the outset, believed in his viability, his competence and ability to steer the Organization in a manner that would regain its status as an institution of excellence. Hence, I supported him and openly campaigned for his election both for the first and second terms in office.

In October 1996, Al-Jarwan invited Hansenne and his family as well as me and my family to visit the UAE. It was a gesture of appreciation for the support and assistance the Office accorded to his candidature.

The visit was touristic for our families. An intensive programme had been prepared for Hansenne and myself. Clearly, the government of the UAE wanted Hansenne to obtain a comprehensive vision of the country's socio-economic development, present and future.

We visited several of the Emirates where we observed the functioning of small-, medium- and large-scale enterprises. We were taken to the Jebel

Ali Free Zone project that was commencing operations, though still in the early stages of its construction. Our programme extended throughout the day with a brief lunch break. On the second day, Hansenne showed signs of discomfort with the intensity of the programme and matters took a more normal and comfortable tempo on the third day.

On the fourth day, Al-Jarwan told me an audience with the Head of State, Sheikh Zayed, was being organized that evening. A farewell dinner was given in honour of Hansenne, who seemed anxious about the timing of his meeting with the Head of State. We were scheduled to leave for Geneva on the next morning and he wished to go to bed early.

Al-Jarwan had indicated to me that he was waiting for a signal from the Presidential Palace. I transmitted this information to Hansenne who was visibly unhappy with the arrangements. It was around 11 o'clock that Al-Jarwan received a call for us to proceed. I accompanied him and Hansenne in the car that led a convoy of several limousines and jeeps.

The journey took nearly 45 minutes, travelling through the desert in almost total darkness. Suddenly a huge structure lit up with the flood lights looming before us. Within minutes we entered the palace grounds and the car stopped at a gate manned by some dozen men dressed in white traditional robes carrying automatic rifles on their shoulders. Throughout the journey, Hansenne, who was sitting in the backseat with me, made several negative remarks about the timing of the audience. Al-Jarwan, who was in the front seat next to the driver, would occasionally turn to request that I apologize to Hansenne for the delay.

When we disembarked, it was evident and imperative that I needed to defuse Hansenne's discomfort and frustration to avoid possible embarrassment. I approached him and while maintaining a serious look quipped, 'With your permission I will inform Sheikh Zayed that you do not approve of the timing of his audiences.'

A huge smile adorned Hansenne's face as we entered the magnificently decorated hall leading to our meeting place. We were directly ushered to a 'salon', where Sheikh Zayed stood, advancing a few steps forward to welcome Hansenne as we approached. The audience lasted for almost half an hour. Sheikh Zayed had a most imposing charismatic character. His remarks centred on the imperativeness of Arab unity and cooperation. He also spoke of the important role that foreign workers played in the construction and development process of the UAE. Sheikh Zayed said it was the duty of this country to make foreign workers feel at home, and to provide them with the salaries, security and respect that were commensurate with their good work.

Hansenne responded by highlighting the role the UAE and Minister Al-Jarwan were playing on the ILO scene and that of the Gulf States vis-à-vis workers' rights and freedoms. He also paid tribute to Sheikh Zayed for his far-sightedness and the mammoth social and economic development the UAE was witnessing under his leadership. As we went out of the meeting, Hansenne's mood had changed entirely. We returned together to the hotel, while Al-Jarwan departed directly to his home.

Contrary to my expectations, Hansenne never referred to my remarks to him at the Palace. He surprised me by not ceasing to speak on our long return journey. He was mesmerized by the character and vision of Sheikh Zayed. Before heading to our rooms, Hansenne looked at his watch. It was nearly two in the morning. With a friendly smile, he said, 'You have to admit they keep unusual working hours in this country.'

I believe Hansenne's personality can best be characterized by his decision to impose a retirement age for Assistant Directors-General at 60. The system had an open-ended age for retirement of ADGs, DDGs and the Director-General.

Hansenne had fallen out in a serious way with the Employers' Group at the ILO. He was convinced that the ADG representing the Employers was the source and cause of that problem. This ADG was approaching the age of 60. Instead of asking the Employers to propose a substitute for him, which was a prerogative of the Director-General, Hansenne took the drastic decision that all ADGs must retire at the age of 60.

He had, in fact, consulted me on this matter before taking his decision. I told him it would be a big mistake, having serious long-term negative ramifications on the Organizations' senior management structure. In effect, his relations with the Employers worsened as a consequence of this action.

As I mentioned earlier, Hansenne was an honest and dedicated man who was alien to the machinations and political complexity of the ILO and its tripartite structure. He was a Director-General that did his utmost to introduce ideas and changes to serve the interest of the Organization. He was a man of vision. Regrettably, his diplomatic, or rather undiplomatic, approach and handling of situations invariably constituted a major stumbling block. I will always cherish working under his leadership and value the excellent work relations we enjoyed. Most of all, I value him for the trust and freedom he accorded to me in managing the Regional Office for Arab States. These were the ingredients that inspired me to excel and to accomplish considerable landmarks in ILO–Arab relations.

The benefits and achievements of our close cooperation are best exemplified in the role we played in building Arab ranks that had been ruptured following Iraq's invasion of Kuwait. Relations between Jordan and the Gulf States had become almost non-existent due to the purported lack of declared support of the Kingdom to Kuwait. With the knowledge and approval of Hansenne, I had actively worked on explaining to Ministers Kuleib, Al-Fayez and Al-Jarwan the need to reconcile all parties concerned, who evidently had considerable interests in common, most of all the labour market. After two years of contacts and consultations, the three Ministers obtained their governments' approval to the proposal I had worked out with the Director-General of the Arab Labour Organization to convene the Arab Labour Conference in Amman.

That event marked the first official interaction between Jordan and the Gulf States. At the time, Prince Zeid was Prime Minister and he made every effort to ensure the success of the event at which King Hussein officiated the opening session. Hansenne was scheduled to attend on the first day. At the last hour, he discovered that his mission programme had inadvertently included a two-day official visit to Turkey on the same date as that of the Arab Labour Conference.

I was already in Amman when I received a telephone call from Hansenne, announcing the conflicting dates in his mission programme. He assured me that he would be with me at the opening ceremony, underlining the importance he attached to participating in that function. Apparently, extensive negotiations were conducted with Turkey whereby Hansenne was provided by a private aircraft to travel to Amman to attend the opening ceremony of the ALC and then return to Istanbul to resume his official visit to that country.

At a private meeting I had with King Hussein and Prince Zeid, they expressed their delight with the arrangements that had been made. They informed me that all the Ministers of Labour of the Gulf States had requested audiences with His Majesty, a sign that relations were progressing in a positive direction. I had also arranged for Hansenne to meet King

Hussein during his fleeting visit. The Director-General embarrassed me by telling the King that I was the best Assistant Director-General at the ILO. Prince Zeid, who attended the meeting, never ceased to tease me, in a friendly manner, over that remark.

Approaching retirement from the ILO

An issue that preoccupied the Gulf Ministers was my succession following retirement. They openly discussed the matter with me, indicating their desire to request Hansenne to retain my services until a 'credible' candidate was identified. At the time, Hansenne, encountering problems with his earlier decision to limit the retirement age of ADGs to 60, had conceded to pressure by the Governing Body to provide extensions of two years in exceptional cases.

Ironically, it was Chotard who as Chairman of the Governing Body requested extension of my contract for two years. He cited as justification the newly established ILO programme for Palestine and the need to ensure a stable and successful transition of the Regional Office that was in the process of resuming its operations from Beirut. The extension was granted. The Gulf Ministers, through Al-Jarwan, sent a letter to Hansenne thanking him for the decision that was in 'the best interest of all parties concerned'. The communication of Al-Jarwan had, in fact, gone further. It informed Hansenne that they would consult with me to identify my successor and present him with a candidature in due course.

I proposed the appointment of a deputy-director, in the person of Taleb Rifai, a Jordanian who was heading a special organization overseeing all foreign aid and investments to Jordan. Prince Zeid, as well as several dignitaries in Jordan, had recommended Rifai. Following in-depth study of his qualifications and experience, Rifai was appointed to the post of Deputy-Director working with me at the Regional Office that had become operational from Beirut.

Consultations had been fully conducted between Hansenne, the Gulf Ministers and I on the appointment of Rifai. It was envisaged that he would succeed me as ADG upon my retirement. As the date of my departure approached, several candidatures were submitted to Hansenne for the post of ADG for the Arab States. The environment revolving around

40. The author at a banquet given in his honour by Lebanese Minister of Labour Adnan Mruweh, on the occasion of his appointment as Director of the ILO Office in Beirut.

41. The author with Director-General Michel Hansenne and his Chief of Cabinet Bill Simpson after being sworn in as Assistant Director-General.

42. Labour Minister of the UAE Saif Al-Jarwan and Under-Secretary Mohamed Al-Sweidi, meeting with the author to discuss Al-Jarwan's candidacy for President of the ILC in 1996.

43. Michel Hansenne and the author meeting with Kuwaiti Foreign Minister (currently Ruler) Sheikh Sabah Al-Ahmad Al-Jaber Al-Sabah, following the end of the Iraqi occupation of Kuwait.

44. Crown Prince Sheikh Saad Al-Abdullah, Minister of Labour Ahmad Kuleib, Michel Hansenne and the author holding discussions on foreign workers.

45. Chairman Yasser Arafat receiving Michel Hansenne at his headquarters in Gaza, with the author in the centre.

46. President Jacques Chirac and Minister Al-Jarwan meeting at the conclusion of the 1996 International Labour Conference, with the author in the centre.

47. The author and Director-General Hansenne escorting HM King Hussein and HM Queen Nour to the Assembly Hall for the royal address to the International Labour Conference in June 1997.

48. Yvon Chotard with the author at the Allenby Bridge, at the start of their official visit to the West Bank.

49. The meeting at which President Hafez Al-Assad of Syria gave a speech attacking Jordan's royal family. The author is first from the right, facing the podium.

50. HM Queen Rania accompanied by Director-General Juan Somavía during her visit to the ILO headquarters, with the author in the centre.

51. Guy Ryder following re-election for second term in office in 2016. From left: Deputy Director-General Greg Vines, Guy Ryder and Chairperson of the Governing Body Ambassador Ulrich Seidenberger (Germany).

that issue became hostile and unwholesome with bitter rivalry among the contesting parties. I was attempting to distance myself from the entire process, which had created serious differences between constituents in West Asia.

One day, I was contacted by the Israeli ambassador in Geneva, Yosef Lamdan, who wished to invite me for lunch. Lamdan and I had made regular contact by virtue of the ILO programme for Palestinians but our encounters had been official and work-oriented. We met at the Hotel La Réserve and were seated on the terrace overlooking the swimming pool and a large park. Following an exchange on numerous general issues that lasted for the duration of our first course, Lamdan asked whether I was definitely retiring by the end of the year. When I replied in the affirmative, he spoke at length about the influence I had had on the Labour Ministers in the Arab States and requested that I intervene in favour of one of the proposed candidates. 'He is a cultured man and would do a very good job,' were his precise words. Politely but firmly I told Lamdan that I considered it inappropriate to interfere in the process of the selection of my successor and that I would in no way be involved in this issue.

Rifai did not get the job. A few months later, he resigned and occupied, in succession, the posts of Minister of Tourism and of Planning in Jordan. After nearly two years, the post of ADG for Arab States became vacant again. Rifai was appointed to it. Following one term in office, he resigned and took the post of Director-General of the World Tourism Organization, a portfolio that he retains to this day.

Contrary to my hopes and expectations, the last 18 months prior to my retirement were among the busiest of my entire career at the ILO. A key element contributing to my super-charged work agenda was the decision taken to re-open the Beirut Office and to move operations back to Lebanon. In fact, the ILO was the first of the UN specialized agencies to resume operations from Beirut. Although the security situation remained 'precarious' according to the UN security evaluation, the Office succumbed to pressure from the Lebanese government, with strong backing from the French government, to move operations back to the field. This entailed considerable negotiations with the local authorities on major issues including the provision of office premises and the question of immunities.

The plan was to implement the move in several phases, over a period of six months, which would allow re-assessment of the security situation. On a personal level, I decided that my family would remain in Geneva in view of my impending retirement. Until that period in time, I literally had no time to give serious thought to my future plans, let alone to take action in this regard.

I was determined to complete the move and ensure that the office was fully operational prior to my retirement. Almost all the officials at the Ministry of Labour, the Ministry of Foreign Affairs, and other concerned government departments, whom I had known prior to the evacuation of the office, had been changed. I found myself in an alien environment wherever I went. To my pleasant surprise, in spite of the changed structures, I received full cooperation at all levels coupled with a friendly and constructive attitude.

Within weeks of my being in Beirut, Chotard paid me a surprise visit. During his short sojourn, I arranged for him to meet the President of the Republic, the Prime Minister, the Ministers of Labour and Foreign Affairs and the representatives of the Workers and Employers. I was pleased with his visit and the keen interest he showed in the work I was doing. To my utter surprise, he asked if I would consider prolonging my stay with the ILO for one more year. He expressed concern about the 'ongoing crises' regarding my succession and the transmission of operations of the Regional Office to Beirut.

I assured Chotard that my decision to depart at the end of 1998 was final and thanked him for his kind offer. I was tempted to ask him whether he had discussed with Hansenne the suggestion he made to me, but refrained from doing so, lest he might interpret that as a sign of possible interest. When I visited Geneva, nearly a month later, I had confirmation from a very reliable source that Chotard had obtained the green light from Hansenne to offer me an extension. My final words to Chotard as he was departing for Geneva were those of assurance and commitment on my part that the Beirut Office would be fully operational prior to my retirement.

In spite of my deep involvement in the affairs of the office and my constant shuffling between Beirut and Geneva to resolve administrative, personal and financial matters, I had one major ambition that I was determined to accomplish prior to my departure.

King Hussein visits the ILO

I wanted to crown my career by having King Hussein of Jordan as guest of honour at the 85th Session of the International Labour Conference to be held in June 1997. The King was a friend for whom I had the highest regard and respect. I wished to arrange this event as a token of appreciation, at the international level, for his wise and visionary leadership over several decades. Yet, perhaps, the root of my motivation and earnest desire for that undertaking was inspired by a sense of deep indebtedness on my part and that of the Palestinian people to the Hashemite Royal Family. They had granted us a new lease of normal life by providing us with nationalities, thereby terminating our spiral of being stateless with all the torment and suffering entailed.

It was an expression of gratitude to king and country for their act of humanity to be recorded in the annals of history. I had mentioned this idea to Hansenne when we attended the Arab Labour Conference in Amman. His initial reaction was positive and I knew that I had to pursue this matter with speed and vigour. Early in 1997, I hand-delivered Hansenne's letter of invitation to King Hussein at the Royal Palace. His Majesty requested me to thank the Director-General and to convey to him his acceptance of the invitation.

It is opportune at this juncture to mention an event that occurred in my early days as Director of the Regional Office in Beirut. I was designated to represent the Director-General at an important meeting in Damascus organized by the influential Syrian Federation of Trade Unions. At that period in time, relations between Syria and Jordan were at their lowest ebb. It was announced that President Assad would deliver an important speech at that gathering.

Upon my arrival at the headquarters of the Syrian Federation of Trade Unions, the venue of the meeting, I was surprised to be escorted to a seat of honour in the first row facing the podium. During the long wait for the arrival of President Assad, hushed rumours were circulating that his speech would focus on Syria's relations with Jordan.

I do not exaggerate when I say that that afternoon was one of the most embarrassing and uncomfortable moments of my entire life. I had to endure listening to President Assad for two hours pouring a stream of endless insults on the King and members of the Jordanian royal family.

His speech was punctuated by endless orchestrated standing ovations that often lasted for several minutes.

In the midst of this emotionally charged environment, my thoughts drifted back in time to the year 1977 when President Assad was the only head of state to attend the funeral of Queen Alia. As already noted, Blanchard and I were present at that sad and moving event. I recall Prince Zeid telling me that President Assad had insisted on attending the burial ceremony, which was principally restricted to family members and local dignitaries. The paradox was striking, illustrating the dramatic and constant change in political affiliations among Arab leaders.

Regrettably I was a victim of a Catch-22 situation, where I could not withdraw and was obliged to be party to a hysterical emotional demonstration alien to all forms, norms and levels of diplomacy. I had planned to go to Jordan on the following day on an official visit and a luncheon with Prince Zeid had been scheduled. I arrived at his home, located on the outskirts of Amman, early in the afternoon and was met with the customary brotherly warm welcome. His wife, Nawzat, joined us and I observed an exchange of looks between them as smiles dawned on their faces.

How well I remember Prince Zeid's words to me, 'His Majesty and I watched the live broadcast of Assad's speech yesterday and we both recognized you sitting in the front row.' He went on to quip jokingly, 'We noted you occasionally applauded, though evidently half-heartedly.' Prince Zeid added that His Majesty, who knew I was lunching with him the following day, told him to tease me about my 'supportive' reaction. Naturally, our discussion during the luncheon centred on the Assad speech and both Prince Zeid and Nawzat consoled me for the unpleasant and uncomfortable experience I had encountered. Reflecting later on this event, I realized that if I had been a national of some of the other Arab countries, the consequences could have been dramatic on me and perhaps even on members of my family.

I will forever remember the afternoon of 12 June 1997 when I was among the group of officials who welcomed King Hussein upon his arrival at Geneva airport. As the royal aircraft approached, we could see the cockpit with His Majesty in the pilot's seat. He was a skilled and seasoned aviator with whom I had the honour and privilege of flying on several occasions in Jordan in our younger days. He was in good spirits and when he reached me a broad smile filled his face. He embraced me, saying in his husky voice, 'Good to see you, Shukri.' The King was accompanied by Queen Nour, the Prime Minister, Abdel Salaam Al-Majali, other ministers and a group of high-ranking officials.

The King's visit was historic in more than one sense. His speech was hailed by the tripartite constituents as one that dealt with core ILO issues with clarity, precision and a futuristic vision. During the 25 ILCs I had attended up until that day, never had there been such enthusiasm and warm reception for any previous guest of honour. The Assembly Hall was literally packed. All galleries, even the diplomatic one, were full with standing room only. His Majesty was received with standing ovations, both when he entered the Assembly Hall and at the end of his speech, ovations that lasted for over five minutes each. When the King and his entourage arrived at the ILO building for the luncheon, the staff members in their hundreds were there to greet him with unceasing applause.

Prior to the lunch, I had arranged for His Majesty to meet with the Ministers of Labour of the West Asian countries. The objective was to give him an opportunity to have one-on-one discussions, particularly with those of the Gulf States. The arrangement worked out extremely well. In fact, His Majesty had long, private talks with Minister Kaleib of Kuwait as well as the Ministers of Saudi Arabia, the UAE and Bahrain.

I cannot but recount an incident that happened immediately following the end of the King's speech. As is customary, the Director-General escorted His Majesty to the large meeting room where he would receive members of the tripartite delegations who wished to meet him as well as diplomats and Jordanian citizens. As soon as the Director-General had taken leave from His Majesty, and prior to allowing visitors to enter the room, the King told me that he wanted to have a cigarette. Smoking is prohibited at the Palais des Nations and certainly in the VIP meeting rooms.

I immediately rushed to the door requesting the security and protocol officials not to allow anyone to enter until I gave them the green light to do so. I returned to His Majesty and informed him that he could smoke but it had to be rapid. I also asked if he could possibly place himself near the window, which I quickly opened to allow the smoke to go out. While he was moving towards the window his face lit up with a broad smile and he asked me, 'Any other orders?'

After the official lunch at the ILO building, we escorted His Majesty and the delegation accompanying him to the airport. He was leaving for

London. Our old Victoria College friend Ghazi Shaker, who resided in London, had planned to give a lunch in honour of the King during his visit. I was invited to that special event and King Hussein was aware of that. While bidding me farewell at Geneva airport, he embraced me and thanked me for all I had done to make his visit a success. His parting words were: 'we will see each other in a few days in London.'

My career beyond the ILO

Little did I know or imagine what that visit to London had in store for me or the effect it would have on my future.

London is a city close to my heart. It is a place where I feel at home. I love its rhythm, tempo and people. It certainly always reminds me of my days at Victoria College and the wonderful teachers whose memories I will forever cherish. I would often visit London, especially when Prince Zeid was there. His presence always presented Ghazi and myself with an opportunity to enjoy every minute of each other's company, while reliving the lovely memories of our school days. I arrived in London a day before the lunch Ghazi was giving in his magnificent country house in honour of King Hussein. Prince Zeid had already been there for a couple of days.

We arranged to have dinner together and although Ghazi and Zeid had their wives in the city we decided it would be a stag get-together. In reality, this arrangement usually suited our wives who were saturated by spending their time listening to our repeated nostalgic memories of our school days.

Sometime during the evening Prince Zeid, recalling that my retirement from the ILO was imminent, asked what my future plans were. I told him that I had been submerged by work to such an extent that I had not given any serious thought to that matter. In a very casual way, he asked whether I would be at all interested in moving to settle in Jordan. He said he was ready to intervene with His Majesty to secure a post for me in the palace or some other appropriate entity. While thanking him, I responded that I had never lived in Jordan and that it would be difficult to uproot my family and children, who were schooling in Geneva. The conversation ended on that note and Ghazi began talking to us at length about his lunch the following day and about the very special arrangements made for the guests numbering over 100.

Suddenly, as though slipping into a trance, my mind drifted away from the conversation and the earlier words of Prince Zeid to me were reverberating in my ears and mind. To my surprise, as though some power had descended upon me, a hitherto totally unknown idea came to my mind. I interrupted the conversation, telling Prince Zeid that I had just thought of a proposal regarding my future, which the King and he could help me realize. I told him I would be ready to work as Counsellor for ILO Affairs at the Jordan Mission in Geneva, without financial remuneration, in return for maintaining my diplomatic status in that capacity.

Both Prince Zeid and Ghazi questioned the logic of working without pay. I explained that being on the pay roll would implicate responsibilities and limit the duration in that post. Initially both mocked me good-humouredly for that explanation. Moments later, Prince Zeid asked whether I was serious about my proposition. When I replied in the affirmative, he and Ghazi agreed that we would seek the opportunity, during lunch the next day, to discuss this matter with the King.

Our plan proved more complicated to execute. Almost all the guests were constantly converging on His Majesty wishing to talk to him or take a photograph. I had almost given up hope when Ghazi accompanied Prince Zeid and myself to where the King was seated and told him that the three of us wished to discuss something in private with him. The people at the table withdrew with speed and a slight embarrassment, sensing they had exceeded their share of time with the King. Prince Zeid told His Majesty about the proposal I had made for my post-retirement activity. The King's immediate reaction was: 'Why be Counsellor and not Ambassador?' I responded by thanking him, while explaining that I did not wish to work full-time and that my objective was to remain in Geneva as long as possible.

I recall his exact words to me, which were, 'If that is what you want, consider it done.' The King then told Prince Zeid to remind him upon their return to Amman to issue the necessary orders. Within weeks, the Royal Decree was issued appointing me Special Counsellor for ILO Affairs at the Jordan Mission. In the same week that I retired from the ILO at the end of 1998, I took up my new post at the mission and remain in that function to date.

Incredible as it may seem, the visit of His Majesty to the ILO and my subsequent meeting with him in London were instrumental in changing the course of my life. The totally improvised idea that dawned upon me at dinner with Prince Zeid and Ghazi is tangible proof of the role fate and destiny can play in one's existence.

That was not the first time that His Majesty demonstrated acknowledgement of my services to Jordan. In October 1992, much to my surprise and pleasure, King Hussein granted me the decoration of 'Al-Kawkab Al Urduni' (Order of the Star of Jordan), an honour which I will deeply cherish forever.

My departure from the ILO in 1998 provoked in me a wave of mixed emotions. Having dedicated 25 years of my prime life to the Organization, it was no easy task to extract myself from an environment that had become an inherent part of my system. The farewell accorded to me by the staff of the Beirut Office, charged by visible expressions of friendly emotions, added to my torment.

Fortunately, the various events and activities that preceded my retirement, spanning a period of several months, were factors that had well prepared me for that moment of reckoning. I was convinced that the timing of my retirement was the ideal one. I had reached the peak of my performance and career. Hence, it was time to part, leaving behind me a successful professional legacy that was acknowledged by the tripartite constituents as well as the successive Directors-General of the ILO. Interestingly all those concerned unanimously attributed this legacy to my ability 'to preserve and protect the interest of the tripartite constituents in the Arab countries while fully upholding and sustaining the standards and values of the ILO'. The fact that I was commencing a new, honorary job that kept me within the sphere of the ILO was an added gratification. Indeed, I looked forward to being a representative of a government, as opposed to my former status as an ILO official.

The transformation in my professional career coincided with a change in the leadership of the ILO. Hansenne's term in office ended in 1998. In 1999, he became a member of the European Parliament – a position which he still holds.

In March 1998, the Governing Body elected Juan Somavía to serve as the ninth Director-General of the ILO. His five-year term of office began on 4 March 1999. Somavía had previously held key positions in the United

Nations including those of President of the United Nations Economic and Social Council and Permanent Representative of Chile on the United Nations Security Council, as well as being President of the Security Council in April 1996 and October 1997.

A seasoned diplomat, who was well acquainted with the United Nations system, Somavía lost no time in introducing radical changes in the management and policy direction of the ILO. He was determined to give more prominence to the ILO at the international level by introducing programmes that would be endorsed and adopted worldwide. In 1999, he submitted his Decent Work Agenda to the International Labour Conference. The Organization adopted 'Decent Work' as the contemporary expression of its historical mandate. The programme was endorsed by the United Nations and its Specialized Agencies and Organizations. In 2002, the ILO created the World Commission on the Social Dimension of Globalization. It was the first official body to take a systematic look at the social dimension of globalization. The programme received wide support from the United Nations to the G20.

During the ILO Global Jobs Summit in 2009, the ILO adopted a Global Jobs Pact designed to guide national and international policies aimed at stimulating economic recovery, generating jobs and providing protection to working people and their families. The Jobs Pact was thereafter welcomed by the leaders of the G20 at the Pittsburgh Summit. This led to the regular and active participation of the ILO at meetings of the G20. The aforementioned are but a few examples of the expansion of the image and presence of the ILO at the international level.

My relations with Somavía developed rapidly and in a very positive manner. He became aware of the active role I was playing within ASPAG and the Arab Group. In fact, he often solicited my support on delicate issues on the agenda of the Governing Body.

Traditionally, Jordan's role in the ILO had been one of a moderator. Within a relatively short period of assuming the post of Counsellor, both the ASPAG and the Arab Group systematically sought my advice and opinion on key subjects, taking into account my long experience as an ILO official and my institutional memory. Simultaneously, the Office regularly consulted with me on major matters to ensure the non-emergence of unexpected problems.

Hence, it was within this context and environment that I commenced my new assignment. While acknowledging the value and benefits of this new status, I was fully aware of the risks and dangers entailed. I had envisaged keeping my new assignment for no more than three to five years, after which time I would fully retire.

It may sound odd or strange, or both, if I were to confess that it was only at this stage of writing my memories that I became aware that 2017 would mark the 18th year of my service with the mission. In fact, I had been oblivious of the fact that I had served with six different ambassadors, the term in office of each being for a duration of three years. My relations with them all were friendly and cordial. They appreciated and valued the work I was performing and constantly paid tribute to my achievements. Unimaginable as it is, I believe the memory lapse I had is the outcome of the very active, interesting, challenging and productive professional atmosphere that engulfed me.

Highlights of my work as Labour Counsellor for Jordan

It is no easy task to portray, let alone select, events that spanned over a period of almost two decades. Hence, I will endeavour to recount some of the highlights of my experiences and achievements during that period, hoping that such an overview will provide a picture of the entire spectrum.

In the year 2000, I succeeded in adding the name of Her Majesty Queen Rania Al-Abdullah of Jordan to the list of ILO first ladies in combating child labour. On 3 October 2002, Her Majesty visited the International Labour Office to meet the ILO Director-General Juan Somavía and other senior officials of the Organization. The visit of Her Majesty, who has a special interest in children's issues, focused on the launching of an expanded programme against child labour in Jordan and on her support for the ILO's campaign against child labour nationally and internationally.

On 12 June 2003, HM King Abdullah II Bin Al-Hussein addressed the 91st session of the International Labour Conference as guest of honour. His Majesty, who was accompanied by Queen Rania, delivered a resounding speech in which he declared that: 'work and working people are at the heart of prosperity.' He told the 2,500 delegates at the Conference that the 'war on want must be won to heal the divisions and despair that feed global violence.'

On that occasion, the royal couple presented the ILO with a gift comprising a traditional carpet from the Beni Hamida tribe together with the weaving machine. Thanks to my good relations and contacts with the ILO senior management, I secured the most prominent site for exhibiting the gift at the entrance of the ILO headquarters. Due to my intervention, the gifts presented by the governments of the United Arab Emirates and Saudi Arabia were also given privileged locations, which they continue to occupy.

I was also instrumental in the appointment of the Jordanian Minister of Labour Nidal Katamine as President of the International Labour Conference (ILC) in 2013 as well as Ambassador Rajab Sukayri, who was Jordan's Permanent Representative in Geneva, as Vice-President of the ILC in 2012. In 2014, I arranged for the Prime Minister of Jordan Abdullah Ensour to address the 103rd session of the ILC on the effects of the Syrian refugees' crisis in Jordan and the country's reform drive. These are but a few of the events that I organized for the participation of high-ranking dignitaries from Jordan in addition to ensuring representation of Jordan in most ILO meetings and events, both at the regional and international levels.

Simultaneously, I actively followed up on securing technical assistance for Jordan from the ILO in the form of projects and activities in favour of the tripartite constituents. In fact, Jordan has enjoyed the highest rate of technical cooperation with the ILO among all countries in West Asia during the past two decades, including fellowships and training programmes. Another key achievement was securing a seat for Jordan at the ILO Governing Body. Having such a status enabled Jordan to play a role and to have a say in the Organization's present and future policies, and provided it with the opportunity to constantly interact with the key member states and coordinate with them action at the national and regional levels.

I should mention that during the past 15 years a dramatic change for the worse has befallen the group of Arab States at the ILO. Admittedly, the Arabs had their traditional differences and divergences. However, more often than not they were united on certain key issues and subjects such as the Palestinian case and cause.

By contrast, the consequences of the invasion of Iraq, the change of regime in Libya, the armed conflicts in Syria and Yemen and the ramifications of the Arab Spring inflicted serious and deepening rifts that abrogated all inter-Arab common cooperation. As a consequence, the Arab group lost its prestige and clout. It became totally fragmented, reshaping itself into small splinter groups, each of which was in search of recognition and protection by totally alien and external bodies.

The grouping of the Arab tripartite constituents was no longer based on principles and ideals but purely on political affiliations. The ICATU was dismantled and replaced by several other unions, each claiming leadership of the Arab workers.

The Gulf countries formed a sub-group under the name of the Gulf Cooperation Council. Other countries like Iraq, Yemen and Syria became like orphans in search of alliances, which varied according to the changing circumstances.

Jordan was the only Arab state that maintained a formidable status within the Arab group and individually. In fact, its neutrality enabled it to play a key role within the Arab group as well as ASPAG.

The total lack of Arab solidarity is best exemplified in an event involving the post of President of the Governing Body of the ILO during the period 2011–12. This post is occupied by a titular member of the GB by rotation among the regional groups.

In 2011, it was the turn of ASPAG to nominate a candidate from its group. I had worked hard for a period of two years to obtain the support of ASPAG as well as that of the Employers' and Workers' groups for Jordan to be nominated in the person of the Ambassador Shehab Madi, the Permanent Representative of the Kingdom in Geneva. Having obtained the endorsement of all concerned and the full blessing of ILO Director-General Juan Somavía, all that remained to be done was for the Arab group to nominate Jordan for the titular seat at the Governing Body – a process that was strictly internal for the West Asian countries. Noteworthy is that such an event would mark the first time ever for an Arab country to occupy the prestigious post of President of the GB.

The Gulf Ministers of Labour held a meeting at which they decided that Qatar should take the titular seat. They were fully aware of Jordan's nomination and that Qatar would not qualify for the Presidency, as it did not have trade unions and the Workers' group would veto its candidature. To add insult to injury, Qatar openly declared that it had no desire or intention to be President of the GB, only to become a titular member of the GB. On several occasions, Ambassador Madi requested the Minister of Labour of Jordan to intervene with his Qatari counterpart. For some obscure reason, no such contact was made and Qatar obtained the titular seat.

Australia, which was not a titular member, expressed its interest in the post to ASPAG. In an act of solidarity, South Korea, which was next in line for the post, conceded its titular seat to Australia to enable its delegate, Greg Vines, who held a ministerial post at its mission in Geneva, to be nominated. A sad historical event that depicts in the most clear terms Arab disunity and antagonism, while other nations were ready and willing to support another country within the larger group for the interest of the region.

Greg was, in fact, a newcomer to the ILO with whom I quickly developed a close friendship. Shortly after his arrival, he was appointed coordinator for ASPAG. He demonstrated an impressive ability to comprehend and deal with that group which comprised the largest and most diversified number of countries.

With time, our work relationship was consolidated and we cooperated as a team to deal with issues pertaining to ASPAG as well as those that concerned ILO policy, including the proposed reform of the Conference and the Governing Body.

I recall the time when the post of Regional Director for Asia and the Pacific became vacant and Greg indicated to me that he was interested in occupying it. The problem was that the said post was traditionally held by a Japanese national. Japan had already presented two candidatures that were rejected by the Director-General.

Working with utmost discretion, I managed to convince ASPAG members that the monopoly of that post by Japan was not in the best interest of the group. Somavía informed me, confidentially, that he would have no problem appointing a non-Japanese, subject to the agreement of the Japanese government. Following intensive discussions with the Japanese delegate to the Governing Body, and in light of the position taken by ASPAG, the Japanese government agreed to forgo its right to the post if its third proposed candidate would be turned down.

Fate and destiny, however, intervened. Greg Vines was appointed President of the Governing Body, following the let-down of Jordan by the Arab Group. In fact, he frequently remarks that he was elected by default thanks to Arab disunity. Greg gained the respect and admiration of the tripartite constituents for the manner in which he conducted the proceedings of the GB.

His presidency coincided with the elections of the Director-General to replace Somavía. It was the first time that there was a deluge of candidates, numbering nine. Greg was charged with the responsibility of setting up an electoral system that was functional and effective – a task which he performed with much success. In fact, what he formulated was a method that later became a model for other UN organizations.

Guy Ryder was elected Director-General and he appointed Greg Vines as Deputy Director-General, a considerably more senior post than that of a Regional Director. I should mention that Guy, Greg and I developed a fairly close professional and personal relationship. We often had lunches or dinners during which the three of us had an exchange of views and ideas on issues pertaining to the ILO, as well as general subjects of interest to us. This tradition continues to this day, with less participation of Guy due to his extensive work and travel programmes. It is worth noting that the open channel of contact between us continues unabated whenever need or cause demands.

While Guy is commencing a new term in office of five years, I am in the process of phasing out. I envisage my total retirement by the end of 2018 or early 2019, a year that would mark the centenary celebrations of the ILO. Guy has made much progress in reforming the ILO during his first term, yet considerable work remains to be done. I believe we have in him a good partner. I look forward to jointly working with him to overcome some serious obstacles that are inherent in a UN system renowned for resisting change. In my opinion, a major issue for change relates to the environment of the ILO and the mentality of its staff. In a world of globalization, where youth employment constitutes a universal crisis, the ILO cannot and should not harbour staff who use and abuse the preferential working conditions of the Organization. The staff union should desist from protecting deadwood and assist the management in demanding from the staff a level and quality of performance commensurate with their remuneration and excellent working conditions.

Change required

Change has to come from within. ILO staff policy should correlate to that of the private sector to enable the Organization to affect its aspired tangible reforms and achievements. This is an area in which I intend to invest considerable time and effort in the coming years in the hope that positive results will be realized.

I believe that while the forthcoming centenary is an occasion to reflect on and appreciate the ILO's past achievements, it should be the juncture and turning point for the Organization to launch a reformed structure and adopt a new vision and policies that would secure for it a leading and prominent role at the international level in future.

The other area to which I intend to dedicate much of my time and work is that of promoting youth employment. I am anguished by the thought and sight of youth who are unable to find employment and are hence denied the opportunity to construct a normal life and future. The ILO is certainly one of the prime vehicles that can assist this tortured generation in its search for jobs and security. I will utilize all my experience, knowledge and contacts within and outside the ILO to promote the cause of youth employment until the day I retire.

In spite of my deep frustration at the disarray among the Arab countries for over a decade, I have never wavered in my efforts to sustain Arab unity and endeavours to maintain the status and prestige of the group.

Looking back and looking forward

In the late 1970s and up to the middle of the 1990s, the Arab world witnessed unprecedented political and military developments that inflicted considerable fragmentation and disarray on member states of the region. The formal peace treaty between Egypt and Israel was concluded in March 1979 and normalization between the two countries went into effect in 1980 when ambassadors were exchanged.

As a consequence, the Arab States severed relations with Egypt. The Arab League was moved to Tunis and all its affiliated organizations were also relocated to other Arab States. A decade later came the Iraqi invasion of Kuwait in August 1990 that was followed by the liberation of the country in February 1991.

These events naturally gave rise to an extremely negative environment among the tripartite Arab constituents at the ILO. Whenever meetings were convened at the national, regional or international levels, participating Arab delegations engaged in heated verbal exchanges among each other that were alien to the subject matter and to customary diplomatic norms.

Needless to say, the utter disunity among the Arabs affected their status in the Organization and seriously hampered the work of the Regional Office for Arab States. It was a period when officials like myself constantly walked on a very tight rope to avoid accusations of bias or favouritism. I considered my role as an objective unifier and constantly urged the Arab tripartite constituents to avoid indulging in open confrontations at international forums such as the ILO.

By and large, my efforts bore fruits. Delegations were ready and willing to engage in private discussions where they would let out their venom. As a consequence, their attitudes towards each other at the meetings and official sessions were restrained with the exception of occasional minor skirmishes. I was fully aware that by taking this stand I would be subjected to situations when I would be accused of conspiring with one entity against another or even being a 'traitor' to the Arab cause, whatever that may mean. My conviction was that I needed to play a role in avoiding the airing of inter-Arab feuds and conflicts at the ILO. I was confident that once tensions eased and common sense prevailed, I would come out of the hostile and stormy environment unscathed, irrespective of the accusations directed to me during the process. In reality, this is exactly what happened. I emerged with a much stronger image and status among all constituents, who appreciated my active and positive involvement in bridging their differences and protecting their image and interest at the international level.

I certainly intend to continue in my mission to support the Arab countries, a task which I assumed early in my career as an ILO official. Within this context, the Palestinian case and cause will continue to occupy a leading and prominent part of my activities.

My experience, contacts and status at the ILO will focus on defending and protecting the interest of Arab governments and in particular those of the Gulf States that seek reform and who remain vulnerable due to the absence in their countries of trade unions and workers' organizations. I will spare no effort in assisting them to develop the structures and legislation that conform to ILO standards.

I will most certainly engage fully in the 'Standards Initiative' to reform, strengthen and improve the supervisory system. I believe a major contribution to the Organization's Centenary would be to establish a transparent and effective supervisory system that would uphold ILO standards while exercising total neutrality and transparency.

The role of the supervisory bodies should be primarily to guide and assist member states to conform to the standards. A friendlier environment must be developed between the supervisory system and member states to enable it to function in the aspired manner.

My ambition is to maintain the image and status I earned for Jordan over several decades as a mediator and moderator at times of crises, always enjoying the respect of the tripartite constituents.

Perhaps a pertinent and appropriate example of my modest contribution to the ILO is best portrayed in an incident that occurred during the debate of the last Programme and Budget presented by Somavía to the Governing Body. There was strong opposition to the proposal by most governments, though it was based on a zero-growth budget.

During the initial debate, Somavía had been requested to make several amendments and cuts to which he responded positively. It was an ironic situation where the constituents demanded a reduction in a zero-growth budget as well as an increase in ILO activities.

I vividly recall spending an entire evening at home to prepare a statement to deliver the next day at the Governing Body in support of the budget. I had meticulously studied the budget and based on my long experience considered it to be reasonable and appropriate.

Before the start of the session, Somavía came to greet me and in his habitual friendly manner said, 'I would very much appreciate it if you could make a statement on the budget.' My reply was in the affirmative. Yet I did not indicate whether or not I would give my support.

My statement was thorough and comprehensive. It provided analyses of the various items while detailing the justification for each of them. As I spoke, I sensed a feeling of interest among the Governing Body members, conspicuous by the silence that prevailed.

Jordan is by no means a major contributor to the ILO budget, nor is it one of the key member states when it comes to political power. Yet my speech had a considerable impact. No sooner had I finished my intervention, when a stream of delegates took the floor to express their support to the budget, many of whom had earlier expressed their opposition. The budget was adopted.

As I was leaving the Governing Body Hall, the ILO Treasurer Greg Johnson came to thank me saying, 'I owe you one.' More significantly, Guy Ryder approached me with a smile on his face. His words remain to resound in my thoughts and memory. He said, 'The ILO is lucky to have a friend like you.'

Throughout my career in the ILO, as an official and later as a government delegate, I sought to serve the interest of the Organization and the member states I represented. My dedication was not to an administration, a system or individuals but to a unique tripartite institution that embodies a conglomerate of principles and standards affecting the basic needs of all humans and universal social justice.

It is most gratifying, at this state and juncture of my career, that I enjoy a strong and profound sense that my mission has been accomplished. If I were to disappear today from the ILO scene, I hope my legacy would be that I was instrumental in strengthening and improving relations between West Asian countries and the Organization, as well as having been the catalyst in initiating a dialogue between the Gulf States and the Arab trade unions. I would like to be remembered as a 'friend' of the Organization, who spared no effort to uphold its principles or fight for its rights.

It is with a feeling of contentment and fulfilment that I hand over the banner to the new generation and am hopeful that the Centenary will give birth to a reformed and rejuvenated ILO, fully capable of facing the challenges of the turbulent future that lies ahead.

Epilogue
The Future Ahead

My initial plan was to conclude my autobiography at this stage. However, I consider that I would be doing injustice to myself, my autobiography and my readers if I did not delve a little into the socio-political environment that prevails throughout the Middle East, Europe and the USA. We are witnessing an unprecedented era where the 'world order' has lost its traditional rules.

Nations, irrespective of their economic or military might, are struggling to deal with their social and economic turbulences, while facing dramatic security uncertainties. Our world is preoccupied by far-right extremism, fundamentalism and Islamophobia. We are observing alliances among adversaries who are drifting further and deeper into conflicts where the enemy is a 'phantom' and the objectives are varying and obscure.

What does the medium- and long-term future bear for us? What are the consequences of the new American era? What toll will be claimed by the changes sweeping throughout Europe in favour of the far right and extremists? Is globalization going to be a prime victim of the changing socio-economic environment?

I do not intend to predict or forecast the outcome of these developments. My main objective is to state facts and pose questions in order to enable readers to draw their own conclusions.

Often, for political reasons, there are serious 'convenient' lapses in the institutional memory of nations. Hence, facts become victim to invented 'fictitious realities' on which public opinion is developed. When dealing with sensitive issues that relate to religion, human lives and human suffering one needs to address the root cause of the problem. Unless this is done, any measures to address such problems would only yield temporary solutions and could be instrumental in fomenting, compounding and complicating the issue rather than solving it.

With the aforementioned backdrop, the amalgam between Islam as a religion and terrorism became a predominant concern in Europe, traversing the Atlantic to install itself equally in America. Never throughout history was any religion profiled as terrorist. Why has Islam been exceptionally singled out at this point in time and for what purpose or cause?

Regrettably, the last two decades witnessed the dismantling of key Arab States. What we have now is a strongly divided, feeble and fragile Arab region, where the majority of leaders are primarily concerned with merely maintaining their control.

The Arabs' hitherto key binding force, Islam, has fallen prey to political feuds. Enmity was fomented between Sunnis and Shias, thereby depleting the remnants of what was a major unifying spiritual affinity and bonding. It is within this tragic reality that Muslims throughout the world find themselves totally impotent to dispel their tarnished image. Here we need to ask: 'Is it just, normal or acceptable, that a Muslim should fear going to pray at the mosque lest he or she be labelled as a fundamentalist or even terrorist?'

When did this presumed trait of 'terrorist' become associated with Arabs and Muslims? Did it exist before the invasion of Iraq, which left in its wake massive destruction, the death of hundreds of thousands of civilians and a state of total chaos that prevails until this day? Are Iraqis, whose security is menaced almost on a daily basis and who lack the basic needs for decent living, content with the imported democracy they were promised? Who could explain that Iraq became the birthplace of ISIS, the so-called Caliphate that emerged 'overnight' to announce its occupation of a major part of the country? One should believe in miracles to imagine that, in our age of satellites and advanced technology, a new nation could be born from within with all its military might and massive following without being detected. Had Iraq not been invaded, could an entity such as ISIS have ever been established?

Libya has become a stronghold of ISIS and Al-Qaida following the deposal of Muammar Gadaffi. All attempts by international and regional powers to bring law and order to that country have failed. The prevailing chaos in Libya has also made it a major uncontrollable route for African refugees seeking jobs and asylum in Europe.

The ongoing war in Syria caused an exodus of millions of refugees to Jordan, Lebanon and some other countries. Jordan and Lebanon, both on the front-line in the fight against ISIS, welcomed the Syrian refugees, despite their limited resources and difficult economic conditions.

In an address to the European Union in Brussels, in 2016, King Abdullah II compared the situation in Jordan, following the influx of Syrian refugees, to having the entire population of Belgium relocated in France. On that occasion, His Majesty significantly stated the need for more interfaith outreach, saying, 'insulting other peoples, and their faith and convictions, is no way forward.'

Is it normal or acceptable that these two countries should carry the brunt of the Syrian human tragedy while other countries known for their principles of democracy and human rights closed their borders, leaving thousands of men, women and children out in the cold? Should the countries that bestowed upon themselves the right to invade and destabilize Iraq, Libya and Syria, under the guise of installing 'imported' democracy, not fully bear the onus of rectifying the consequential humanitarian tragedy of their acts?

Here we should ask ourselves whether Brexit was a direct consequence of the refugee crises that Britain and Europe faced at the time. Will the executive orders on immigration recently signed by President Trump resolve the security fears of America or will they compound the situation and complicate the issue? Why are there deaf ears to statements made by credible officials such as the Swedish Minister of Manpower, who ascertained that despite the considerable number of refugees entering her country, the crime rate had diminished? She strongly rejected the allegations linking refugees to crime and terrorism.

Regrettably, the tsunami that has swept throughout Europe and America profiling Muslims and Arabs as criminals and terrorists has already gained a solid hold in the minds of the masses. Many of these countries – including several with large communities of such profiled citizens – are now openly expressing their rejection of Arabs and Muslims. It is most alarming that the aforementioned trend continues to gain momentum and popular support in Europe and America. We are heading into uncharted territory, taking a leap into the unknown. The danger and fear is that governments, who have not been firm in applying the basic principles of human rights, will be unable to hold the reins of the forces they have wantonly allowed to be unleashed.

Ironically, terrorism is not alien to Europe or America. Italy had the Red Brigades, the largest and longest-lasting left-wing terrorist group, whose action, over a period of more than ten years, claimed the lives of hundreds of people, including that of a former prime minister, Aldo Moro. During the years 1968–77, Germany lived in fear because of the terrorist groups of the Red Army Faction (RAF) and the Baader-Meinhof Group. Spain's ETA terrorist group, according to Spanish government estimates, has carried out over 1,600 terrorist attacks targeting tourists, train stations, football stadiums and even plotting to assassinate King Juan Carlos. There is also the Irish Republican Army (IRA) to mention but a few of the terrorist groups in Europe.

As to America, home-grown terrorism is best exemplified in the car bombing of the Alfred P. Murrah Federal Building in Oklahoma City on 19 April 1995 by two American nationals, Timothy McVeigh and Terry Nichols. The bombing destroyed one-third of the building, killing 168 people and injuring more than 680 others. The blast destroyed or damaged 324 other buildings and destroyed or burned 86 cars, causing an estimated damage worth US$652 million. McVeigh, a US Militia Movement sympathizer, was a Gulf War veteran.

On 2 October 2017, an American by the name of Stephen Paddock opened fire from automatic rifles on thousands of people attending an open-air country music concert in Las Vegas. He killed 58 persons and wounded more than 500 others in the bloodiest act of terror in modern US history. Paddock, who was entrenched on the 32nd floor of the Mandalay Bay Hotel, had stockpiled 23 assault rifles in his room. It took him less than 15 minutes to execute the massacre. He then killed himself, leaving behind the mystery as to the motive for his heinous crime. Acts of terror, in fact, are a prevalent trait that regularly occur in the US. Had the Las Vegas gunman been a Muslim, what drastic and dramatic action would have been taken against his country of origin and, more importantly, what further degradation would have been inflicted on Islam worldwide?

In light of the aforementioned realities, the question that needs to be answered is: how many terrorist organizations existed in the 1960s and 1970s in the Arab and Muslim world and how many acts of terrorism did they undertake in Europe or America? Is it a coincidence that Arab terrorism in Europe and America came into existence following the invasion of Iraq, the toppling of Gadaffi in Libya and the war in Syria?

What about Palestine, the country that remains to herald the longest military occupation in history, lasting more than five decades? What kind of sentiments and attitude can we expect from the Palestinians, who have lived and grown in an environment of bloodshed and destruction, towards their occupiers and those who continue to support them? Should their acts of resistance to the occupation be labelled as terrorist or as liberation in conformity with international law?

This strange environment of Islamophobia that is dawning over Europe and America made me indulge in a process of soul searching. I could not but wonder what would have become of me had I been doomed to remain as a refugee spending my life in a camp with neither hope nor aspiration for a better future or life. What kind of character-moulding would I have acquired as a result of the suffering and deprivation? Could I ever have developed into what I pride myself with today, as an individual who upholds the principles of human rights, democracy and freedom? Would my children and grandchildren ever have had the opportunity to be raised in an environment of peace? Could they ever have had the opportunity of obtaining a good education and most of all live in dignity remote from humiliation? Suffice to say I shudder at the thought of what could have been.

If we answered all the questions posed earlier in a totally objective manner, a clear vision would emerge, embodying realities that are the core of the problems. It is neither by waging wars nor by invading countries nor by advocating Islamophobia that we can rid ourselves of the plague of terrorism. We need to address the problem at its source. Democracy will effectively prevail only when it is home-grown and not when it is imported and imposed. The most ardent enemy of humanity is the application of democracy with double standards. Such practice does not only tarnish the image of democracy but it also leaves a residue of deep-rooted malice and sense of betrayal.

In our world of today, neither building walls nor military might can provide lasting security for nations. Peace and security will prevail only when the sovereignty of nations is respected and populations are left to deal with and determine their own destinies without external interference. It is imperative to re-establish the stability and rule of law in countries that were dismantled by external forces. This is a prerequisite antidote against terrorism, extremism and fundamentalism.

Recently, I was at a dinner where I met a prominent Israeli business-man, who knew I was Palestinian by origin. We had a long discussion on the Palestinian–Israeli conflict, at the end of which he asked if I had a feeling of vengeance towards Israel. My reply was spontaneous and sincere, 'It is not vengeance but justice that I seek.'

Much as I would like to, I am too realistic to advocate utopia. My ardent hope, however, is that the two peoples who are descendants of Ibrahim, Isaac and Ismail, to whom God according to Genesis promised this land, can resolve their differences, heal their wounds and live in peace and harmony in the Holy Land.

Index

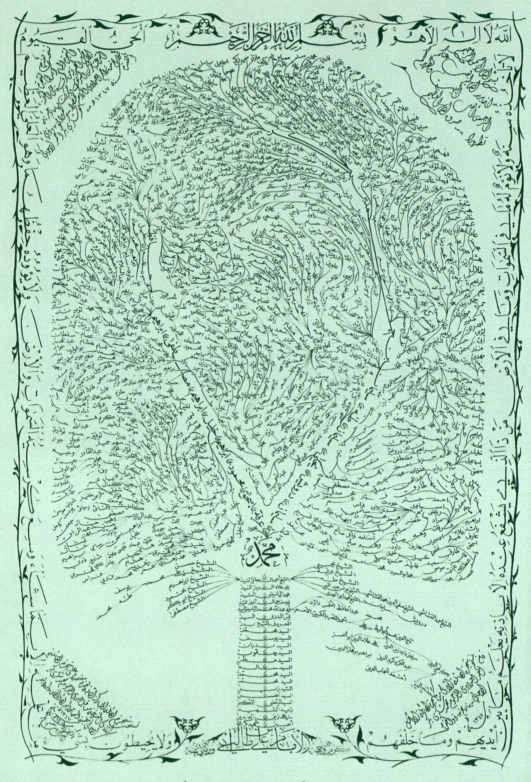

Al-Dajani Family Tree